Jakarta Bites

Exploring vibrant street food from the heart of Indonesia

Jakarta Bites

Exploring vibrant street food from the heart of Indonesia

Petty Elliott

Contents

12 Introduction

24 Ingredients

32 Conversion Table and Basic Information

Betawi Cuisine

40 Starters

58 Soto, Soup, Laksa and Rice

70 Meat, Poultry and Fish

Iconic Regional Dishes Featured Among Jakarta's Food Vendors

82 Seafood

100 Rice, Noodles, Laksa and Soto

126 Salad and Savoury Combinations

146 Meat and Poultry

170 Sate Republic

182 Juices, Sweets and Drinks

This edition published by
Komunika Partners 2016

Copyright
© Petty Elliott 2016

Photography copyright
Komunika Partners 2016

ISBN 978-602-95717-1-4

Printed in Jakarta

for Nick, Christopher and Jeremy

About the Author

Moving to Jakarta from Manado, North Sulawesi, while still in my early teens gave me a wonderful opportunity to sample and enjoy the array of foods available in Indonesia's capital. The culinary complexity, the melding of established traditions with new ideas and trends in a rapidly changing city proved fascinating. In my 'new' home I found that Jakartans enjoyed their own distinctive street food alongside famous recipes from different regions across Indonesia. Good Chinese food was available in parts of the city such as Pasar Baru, Glodok and Pecenongan, alongside international cuisine.

Jakarta was a very different place back then. It featured only a couple of big hotels, hardly any shopping malls and best of all, no traffic. It also proved a good hunting ground for discovering new tastes and the beginning of my own food journey. Jakarta is now a megacity, offering an array of food from traditional dishes to creations from international top chefs, from 'kaki lima' food carts to fine restaurants.

Although my family background is from the city of Manado, at the northern end of the island of Sulawesi far from Java, my mother was actually born in Jakarta and grew up there. She speaks the local Betawi dialect and through her I gained a passion for Betawi cuisine - the fare of old Batavia, as known by the Dutch. "Betawi" was coined in the 18th century, before the modern appellation of Jakarta. It's a pity traditional food is not better known, having fallen to a large extent into the shadow of the many regional and international influences imported into the capital. Betawi cuisine combines local as well as outside influences from visitors past, including Arabs, Indians, Chinese and Europeans.

Indeed, in contrast to Bangkok, Penang or Singapore, Jakarta is a city that seems almost reluctant to reveal its street food secrets.

A giant metropolitan sprawl, it is a magnet for many workers flooding in from the provinces. The local wandering food purveyor proves a welcome sight after a long hard day. Variety abounds in accordance with each vendor's special recipe but also relates to specific districts, for example, where many Chinese-Indonesians have settled.

I cannot recreate the complete experience, the sights and sounds of Jakarta's street food, but I can bring you flavours to stimulate your imagination as well as your palette. The recipes in this book are in many cases my own interpretation of Betawi street food, as I have tried to be faithful but practical. It is clear that knowledge is not always passed on from generation to generation. As incomes rise, so do the temptations of global fast food brands – I guess that's progress – but all the more reason to complete this book as some kind of record of past simpler pleasures.

For over 10 years I have been writing about food in local newspapers and magazines, as well as giving cooking demonstrations and consultations for many five star establishments in Jakarta and Bali. It has been a time filled with the privilege and pleasure of collaborating with many. As I assembled ideas and research for this book, such collaboration included interviewing and learning from both local and international chefs, too numerous to thank individually, It has also been a fascinating re-discovery of the city where I grew up with its many secrets, sights, sounds and aromas of local markets. I hope it represents a worthy tribute to Betawi people and it is certainly a great way to share Jakarta's traditional tastes with you.

Selamat makan,

Petty Elliott

Jakarta, June 2016

Introduction

Jakarta is the gateway to the many delightful flavours of Indonesian cuisine. Every year Indonesia's capital city is a magnet for food vendors from across the archipeplago making it a heaven for foodies.... if you know where to go.

Petty Elliott is both guide and translator of food traditions into exquisite offerings to stimulate the palette.

Jakarta is home to over 10 million inhabitants within the city centre, rising to over 25 million if you include suburban areas. Every day, nearly 1.5 million make the commute to glittering office towers and a large proportion of them can be found lining up for street food, morning, noon and evening.

Those of us living in this vast urban jungle maintain a love-hate relationship with the city. We hate the chronic traffic congestion, yet love the informality and the many convenient services, including access to an almost endless variety of food. No need to travel across 17,000 islands in search of new tastes, you can sample regional Indonesian cuisine on your doorstep, literally. This includes specialities from Aceh at the northern tip of the vast island of Sumatera, the delights of Padang food, a spectrum of Javanese dishes, beautiful and delicate Balinese flavours and famous Manadonese spices.

As a global city, Jakarta offers world cuisine and in my view one of the most diverse and most authentic ranges of Japanese food, outside Japan of course - a reflection of the many Japanese people living and working here. Koreans are aplenty too, as the largest expatriate population in the country. There are some delightful Italian and French cuisines, with European émigré chefs adding interest and variety to their national menus using fresh local Indonesian ingredients. And let's not forget the Dutch influence. The Jakarta food experience is a melting pot of ideas, combining flavours of the world with those of the world's largest archipelago.

I have been living in Jakarta over 30 years and in my heart the 'Big Durian,' as it is affectionately known, is a very special place. Indonesians are polite and deferential, eager to please, and oh so self-effacing. Such character traits may well explain why so few of our visitors know much about Betawi cuisine and street food, as locals assume foreigners would not be interested!

Like other major cities in the region, Jakarta has thrived on change, especially in the hospitality and food industry. Thirty years ago we had only one major supermarket. Today we have endless choices from 'hypers' to minimarts, from specialty meat and fruit stores to 24/7 convenience stores. Twenty years ago, the best restaurants were mainly found in five star hotels run by international hotel groups. Now a vast range of independent restaurants offer outstanding alternatives, with many of them owned by a generation of young local entrepreneurs with palettes honed during study in the USA or Europe.

Previous page: Fatahillah Museum building.

Left: Selamat Datang Monument, in the center of the roundabout *Bundaran Hotel Indonesia.*

Conditions in traditional markets have improved beyond recognition, with good quality local produce. There is room for improvement in support of many local farmers and concepts such as the real artisanal farmers' markets as available in Australasia, Europe and North America, have not yet developed. Nonetheless, we have a superb wealth of indigenous products from palm sugar to rice, from local exotic fruits to the very spices that first brought European ships here, creating fortunes for the merchants who backed them, and a colonial chapter in our past.

As with my first book, Papaya Flower, this volume focuses on Indonesian culinary traditions. The impact of outside influences is a common theme. How many visitors realize that rice cultivation was an imported idea? Before the arrival of rice, cassava was a typical staple. And spare a thought for Indonesian farm incomes, since the main ingredient of the instant wheat noodle, almost a daily modern habit, is almost impossible to grow in our tropical climate. How many have forgotten that cooking with coconut oil, not palm oil, used to be the rule in every kitchen, not the exception? In the context of continuing change, this book if nothing else is an attempt to record Betawi cuisine and Jakarta street food and, with luck, to provide the inspiration to see it survive a little longer, adapting to modern kitchens, without losing its distinctive difference. I offer this glimpse into a hidden treasure trove of taste, exotic ingredients and food ideas.

Betawi Cuisine

As already mentioned, contemporary Betawi cuisine is a mix of local, outside influences and modern realities. Our national footprint is as wide as the widest point of continental North America, embracing three time zones and we are incredibly ethnically diverse – an insight into the variety of our foods in itself. Among 252 million residents, 140 million speak Bahasa indonesia as a second language, with 700 different dialects currently in use. Indonesia is a major crossroads in Asia-Pacific, so little wonder then that Jakarta, as capital and largest port, is a melting pot of tastes.

Modern realities are revealing. Contrarily, given its birthplace by the sea, there are surprisingly few seafood dishes in Betawi cuisine. Some classics like ikan gabus and ikan gurame were actually developed using fresh water fish rather than sea caught varieties. But even here there are issues; the poor condition of local rivers threatens the continuity of supplies of these ingredients. Seafood does features often, but as a minor ingredient; for example, dried shrimp gives a special edge to one of my favourite Betawi dishes 'kerak telur.' You may struggle to find this dish served by local restaurants but it is a real winner at sidewalk food stalls and it inspired me to develop a starter with a modern twist which you can find on page 54.

Asinan Betawi, a fruit and vegetable pickle served with spicy peanut sauce offers a refreshing, light taste, while Sayur Asem is a distinctive sour vegetable soup with young tamarind. Betawi cuisine uses a variety of meats, many secondary cuts as well as tripe and oxtail. Indonesian regional favourites are well represented. Gado-gado (mixed vegetables with peanut sauce) is famous across the whole of Java while Nasi Uduk is a close cousin to Malaysia's Nasi Lemak. Trying to delve into the detail on how and when these influences first arrived, one discovers how little has been written about Betawi cuisine. Like its home, this cuisine has simply evolved from the influences of waves of traders and colonialists over the centuries.

A stir fried beans sprout vendor.

Jakarta's Kaki Lima Food Carts

Many of the recipes in this book have been developed from the offerings of the wandering food vendor. Jakarta's kaki lima, (meaning literally 'five legs') describes the two wheels of the moveable food cart, the third leg used as a prop and the other two legs belonging to the purveyor operating it. They ply the back streets and lanes with distinctive calls to announce their presence, offering a solid meal at a very affordable price.

The Recipes

The process of writing this book provided a great opportunity to help preserve the core of Betawi taste through adaptation and substitution in the modern kitchen. Combining specific ingredients and modern cooking techniques I hope I have succeeded in demonstrating that you can create fine food efficiently from past traditions. It has been a fun way to celebrate local dishes with friends and family gaining insights about culture and people. As the value of spices and herbs has endured for hundreds of years, it seems worthwhile to preserve the unique taste of their place of origin.

Typical Betawi meals comprise several dishes all served at the same time, including rice, vegetables and chicken or tempe, soya cake and tofu. There are no rules so the serving style is entirely your choice. You can follow the all-at-once presentation, or be creative with a succession of courses that contrast one another, or perhaps try serving in a 'spanish tapas style', for fun. Betawi food is enjoyable accompanied by light, dry or even semi-sweet white wines including sauvignon Blanc, Chardonnay and Riesling.

I have stayed broadly loyal to local ingredients but with a hint of outside influences to provide some variety.

Cook's note:
- Unless specified, all cup and spoon measures are level, not heaped
- Eggs are medium sized with an average weight of 60 grammes
- Unless specified, recipes use all purpose flour
- If fresh ginger and turmeric are not on hand you can use 1-2 teaspoon (tsp) of the dried ingredient
- Oven temperatures quoted are for conventional ovens, and need to be adjusted for fan-ovens

Traditional 'Kerak Telur' Betawi omelette vendor.

Some Historical Context

The complexity and flavours of Betawi food result from a rich past as a trading centre with the influence of the many visitors to these shores. With apologies to all historians, here is a very brief summary of Jakarta's colourful past – my own cook's tour, in fact. Stepping far back in time, around the 15th century, Chinese merchants heading through the Malacca strait started visiting these islands on a regular basis. Traders from India brought Hinduism and Buddhism in the 16th century, but only when the first European ships arrived, led by the Portuguese in 1513, does any written detail emerge.

At that time Jakarta was known as Sunda Kelapa, the port town for the Hindu kingdom of Pajajaran. The Hindus signed a deal allowing the Portuguese a presence in the area, a chance for the Hindus to build some influence against a backdrop of Islamic sultanates. But before the Portuguese could establish a proper foothold, Fatahillah of the Banten Sultanate destroyed Sunda Kelapa in 1527 and then founded Jayakarta – meaning Victorious City. The Dutch came ashore in 1596 and established an outpost for the VOC (the Dutch East Indies trading Company) to trade spices, a pivotal point in Indonesian history. At that time, urban Jayakarta was a settlement of only around 3,000 houses.

Left: Sunda Kelapa harbour.

Right: Fatahillah Museum tower.

The British weren't too far behind, settling in around 1615 but not for long. By 1619, the Dutch were back in charge, General Ian Pieterszoon Coen defeated the Sultan of Banten, destroyed his city and rebuilt it with a castle at the center. He chose yet another name, this time in remembrance of the Batavian tribe – ancestors of the Dutch. The name stuck for the next 300 years.

In 1650, Chinese temples went up in Glodok and Ancol on the northern shore, and in 1710, the City Hall at Fatahillah Square. In 1730, the unfortunate inhabitants of Batavia were being so badly ravaged by malaria, there was a mass exodus southward for somewhere more inhabitable. In 1796, the British were back and in 1799 the era of the VOC had ended.

Sir Stamford Raffles, Lieutenant Governor of Java ruled from 1811 to 1815 and was famous for his efforts to push for an end to slavery across the country. The Dutch

returned and their rule lasted until the Japanese arrived in 1942 by which time the city's name Jayakarta was shortened Djakarta or Jakarta.

After the Japanese surrender Indonesia declared de-facto independence, to rebuff further colonial plans by the Dutch and after four years of conflict the Dutch capitulated and modern Indonesia was born. The population of Jakarta at the time was less than 1 million with Kebayoran Baru, the newest neighborhood.

Founding President Sukarno had a grand vision of modernity for his newly freed city, and he set about it with determination, building Istiqlal Mosque, Gelora Bung Karno sports stadium and the 'national monument' Monas. These landmarks and Jakarta's famous and dramatic statues were connected by Jalan M. H. Thamrin running north-south and by Jalan Jenderal Gatot Subroto east–west through the middle of the city. I am sure President Sukarno would be devastated to see what we have done with his original city plans, which demonstrated great vision. His fall from power in 1965 and the emergence of President Suharto saw the job of running the city given to Lieutenant General Ali Sadikin who at the time, stayed true to effective modernization and proper planning.

Things were to change unfortunately. The ensuing resource booms and economic development were highly successful in addressing poverty and paving the way to middle income status. Yet somehow pavements to walk on, a decent public transport system, piped water, a proper citywide sewerage system and green space to suck up rising airborne pollution, got lost along the way.

Today, many of the old streets and their vendors are still there, but squeezed almost to death as glittering malls, hi-rise towers and the spread of the motorcar now rule. Many Betawi people have moved out to ever-sprawling suburbs and new towns across the surrounding coastal plain – from clustered gated communities to rows of neon lit shop houses. Places such as Kemang, Senopati and Sudirman Central Business District have become major destinations for foodies in south Jakarta while Pantai Indah Kapuk (Pik) offers yet more in the north of the city. Maybe the modern planners of these new food heavens will reserve pleasant places to enjoy street food. I hope so.

"Jajanan pasar"
Sweets and cakes
vendor.

Ingredients

The ingredients below are generally listed alphabetically using English – with Indonesian terms added.

1. **Avocado,** *Avokad, Alpokad*
   Butter avocadoes have a smooth, green and shiny skin.

2. **Banana,** *Pisang*
   There are over 300 different types of banana in Indonesia.

3. **Black Pepper,** *Lada Hitam*
   Available widely. Fermented and sun-dried from green, the peppercorns turn hard, black and wrinkled. Interestingly many Indonesian dishes call for white pepper but I prefer in general to use black pepper as it has more fragrance.

4. **Candlenuts,** *Kemiri*
   A very strong flavour and best not eaten raw, Candlenuts are a useful thickening agent. You can substitute macadamia nuts or almonds if candlenuts are not available.

5. **Cardamom,** *Kapulaga*
   This is an important ingredient in recipes from Sumatera, especially curries. White cardamoms are round, differentiating them from the oval shaped green variety grown in India.

6. **Chilli,** *Cabe*
   Indonesian chillies are from the same family as the birds eye chilli and renowned for their fiery bite. The flesh is thin, in colours ranging from deep red and orange to pale yellow. Larger chillies such as the papaya chilli and the long curly chilli, have less heat.

7. **Cinnamon,** *Kayu Manis*
   Sadly, despite its abundance locally, cinnamon is seldom used in Indonesian cooking. Europeans love the warm woody fragrance, both delicate and intense, especially associated with Christmas celebrations.

8. **Cloves,** *Cengkeh*
   Cloves are the unopened flower buds of the syzgium aromaticum or eugenia cayophyllis tree, with an assertive, dark aroma, a warming and rich ingredient in food, drinks and tobacco.

9. **Coconut,** *Kelapa*
   Widespread throughout Indonesia the coconut is an important commodity – as a refreshing beverage, eaten raw or cooked and the meat can be dried. Coconut dried husks make great fuel for barbecues, the timber is used for housing construction, the fronds woven into mats and baskets or used for roof thatch. Mature grated coconut is pressed for coconut milk and coconut oil.

10. **Coconut Cream and Coconut Milk,** *Santan*
    It is easier to buy the canned variety. But if you have the time and desire, crack a mature coconut, grate the flesh into a mixing bowl, adding 200ml of warm water, mix well. Squeeze the mixture with your hands then strain for ready-to-use fresh coconut milk. Alternatively, put the flesh in a juicer for fresh coconut extract.

11. **Coconut Oil,** *Minyak Kelapa*
    This was the traditional cooking oil before the palm oil boom. I prefer soya oil for sautéing and deep-frying.

12. **Fennel,** *Adas Manis*
    Another important ingredient in Acehnese curry and noodle dishes, with a warm and distinctive fragrant similar to star anise.

13. **Fenugreek,** *Klabet*
    The seed has a hard texture and a sweet, curry-like fragrance when roasted. A key ingredient in curry powder and an important spice in Aceh and Sumatera especially in the well-known Aceh noodles.

14. **Finger sour carambola,** *Asam Sunti* **– Dried** *belimbing wuluh (left picture)*
    This is favourite ingredient in Aceh cuisine, North Sumatera. It is belimbing wuluh sliced, salted and dried in the sun. Otherwise known as bottle shape star fruit and sometimes called belimbing sayur or vegetable star fruit. It has an intense sour and salty flavor, is light brown in colour and used in curry, sambals or soups.

15. **Galangal,** *Lengkuas, Laos*
    A member of the ginger family galangal is harder than ginger with a sharper, slightly lemony flavour. The skin is lighter with small pink tips.

16. Ginger, *Jahe*
Both red and white ginger are grown in Indonesia, the red having a smoother texture and sweeter flavour. Combining ginger with chillies and shallots makes a wonderful condiment for any meat.

17. Ginger flower, *Kecombrang*
A young fine flower, native across South East Asia, also known as honje, torch ginger or simply ginger flower. It is an important ingredient in the North Sumatera 'arsik' dish of stewed carp with spices such as andaliman or szechuan pepper. In Kalimantan it is popular for use in sambal pirik. It is a beautiful pink with a delicate and wonderful fragrance. Try to select flowers not fully bloomed for a less fibrous texture. Good for baking, salads and beverages and wonderful for sorbet.

18. Lemon Grass, *Sereh*
Lemon grass provides the intense tangy freshness in so many dishes in the region. The long butter-coloured stems need to be crushed before cooking to release the oil. Add hot water for tea, or mix with limejuice, sugar syrup and ice for a cool refreshing drink.

19. Lesser Galangal/Aromatic Ginger, *Kencur*
A distinctive aroma, quite different from ginger and a little stronger than galangal. Used extensively in Bali and West Java.

20. Chinese Lemon, Calamansi, *Lemon Cina, Lemong cui*
A refreshing, sharp tasting citrus fruit, also used frequently in Filipino and Vietnamese cooking. It makes a good marinade for seafood, added to chilli sauce, and can be mixed with water and sugar syrup for a cool drink.

21. Lime, *Jeruk Nipis*
Well-known in Thai cooking and widely used in Indonesia.

22. Kaffir Lime, *Jeruk Limo*
King among citrus fruits, the kaffir lime has a wonderful fragrance but not much juice. Very good for flavouring fish dishes.

23. Kaffir Lime Leaf, *Daun Jeruk Limo*
These fragrant leaves are essential in most Manadonese dishes. Dried leaves may be substituted if fresh ones are not available. If you have no access to lime leaves in any form, try grating the outer skin of a lime into zest as a good substitute. Packs of fresh lime leaves can be kept in the freezer and used when needed.

24. Mango, *Mangga*
Many different types abound, from egg-sized mangga telur, to mangoes the size of a small papaya, known as mangga kwini used extensively for drinks, salads and desserts. The green unripe mango is great in salad. For easy peeling stand the ripe mango on its end and slice vertically two centimeters on either side of the stone. You can now scoop the mango from its skin with a spoon.

25. Mangosteen, *Manggis*
Sweet white flesh is enclosed in a thick reddish-brown skin. This is a relative of the lychee family and is delicious in salads. Tinned lychees are an acceptable option.

26. Nutmeg and Mace, *Pala and Bunga Pala*
Native to the Banda islands in the Moluccas nutmeg and mace are both parts of the fruit from the nutmeg tree *myristica frangrans*; the fruit contains a nutmeg kernel which is ground or grated while mace are the threads that cover the dried fruit and are also chopped or ground. Both have warm, rich, fresh aromas; though nutmeg has a sweeter taste. The flesh of the fruit is pale, resembling an apricot and is used to make sweet and hot pickles.

27. Palm Sugar, *Gula Aren*
Harvested from a specific palmyra tree. A sweet and watery sap that drips from cut flower buds is heated until thickened and placed in coconut shell to set hard.

28. Black nut, "Pangium Edule", *Kluwak*
These nuts come from the kepayang tree, Pangium Edule of Indonesia, a member of the flacourtia family (Flacourtiaceae). The oily, hard-shelled seeds superficially resemble Brazil nuts but are only edible after soaking and boiling them in water. Fermented kluwak nuts become chocolate-brown and very slippery. Cooked seeds are used in a number of popular Indonesian dishes.

29. Papaya, *Pepaya*
A yellow or reddish skin indicates the ripeness of the papaya, or pawpaw and the flesh varies from yellow, pink and orange. Add lime juice and sugar syrup to create a beverage and it is excellent as a salsa with added ginger, chilli, lime and shallots.

30. Pineapple, *Nanas*
When buying pineapple, choose a sweet fragrant fruit with fresh looking green leaves. Stand the fruit upright and cut the skin one centimeter deep, gouge out the black dots with the tip of your knife. Delicious also in salads; rub with salt to get the best flavour.

31. **Pumpkin,** *Labu Kuning*
Coming in many different shapes, pumpkins can be stored for months if you keep them whole retaining the stems. Known also as butternut squash.

32. **Salted Fish,** *Ikan Asin*
Unsurprisingly there are many varieties of salted fish available in Indonesia. Anchovies are a good substitute.

33. **Screwpine Leaf,** *Daun Pandan*
This leaf gives cakes, drinks and rice a pleasant fragrance and is used as a natural colouring - a vivid unusual green.

34. **Shallot,** *Bawang Merah*
Widely used in Indonesian and Betawinese cooking, offering a sweeter and more delicate flavour than onions.

35. **Shrimp Paste,** *Terasi*
This has a similar function as fish sauce in Thai cooking but carries a stronger smell and flavor. It is essential to roast the shrimp paste before using.

36. **Sour finger carambola**
Also known as star fruit, belimbing sayur or belimbing wuluh it has a fresh sour taste and used in curry or soups. See also Asam Sunti.

37. **Sweet Soya Sauce,** *Kecap Manis*
A very important ingredient in traditional and modern indonesian cooking in sweet and salty varieties.

38. **Star Anis,** *Bunga pekak*
A pungent licorice-like and distinct taste ad a favourite in Sumateran dishes.

39. **Sweet Potato,** *Ubi*
All three varieties of sweet potato: white, red and purple are used for savoury dishes as well as desserts. Can be roasted or added to curries and pies.

40. **Tamarind,** *Asam Jawa*
Widely used by the Javanese the sour tamarind is a perfect combination with palm sugar and chillies. It carries a slightly sweet aroma if the tamarind paste is made from ripe tamarind pods. Ready to use tamarind blocks are available in supermarkets.

41. **Turmeric,** *Kunyit*
Slightly aromatic, with a pungent, bitter, musky taste.

42. **Turmeric Leaf,** *Daun Kunyit*
Used to wrap and flavour fish and chicken when cooked using banana leaves.

43. **Water Apple,** *Jambu Air*
Prettily-coloured fruits are juicy with a light perfume.

44. **White Pepper,** *Lada putih*
Ripe pepper berries then soaked in water, the outer skins removed and the grey inner peppercorns are dried until they turn completely off white. Very commonly used in Indonesian cooking.

45. **Vanilla Pods,** *Vanili*
Once you have tasted real vanilla from a pod, you will never want to go back to synthetic or processed vanilla again.

Conversion Table

Weight

10 g	¼ oz
15 g	½ oz
30 g	1 oz
50 g	1¾ oz
75 g	2¾ oz
100 g	3½ oz
150 g	5½ oz
175 g	6 oz
200 g	7 oz
225 g	8 oz
250 g	8¾ oz
275 g	9¾ oz
300 g	10½ oz
350 g	12¼ oz
375 g	13 oz
400 g	14 oz
425 g	15 oz
450 g	1 lb
500 g	1 lb 2 oz
700 g	1½ lb
750 g	1 lb 12 oz
1 kg	2¼ lb
1.25 kg	2 lb 12 oz
1.5 kg	3 lb 5 oz
2 kg	4½ lb
2.25 kg	5 lb
2.5 kg	5½ lb
3 kg	6½ lb

Volume

1.25 ml	¼ tsp
2.5 ml	½ tsp
5 ml	1 tsp
15 ml	1 tbsp
30 ml	1 fl oz
50 ml	2 fl oz
100 ml	3½ fl oz
150 ml	5 fl ¼ pint
200 ml	7 fl ¼ pint
300 ml	10 fl ½ pint
500 ml	18 fl
600 ml	20 fl 1 pint
700 ml	1¼ pints
850 ml	1½ pints
1 litre	1¾ pints
1.2 litres	2 pints

tsp – teaspoon

tbsp – tablespoon

Measurement

3 mm	⅛ in
5 mm	¼ in
1 cm	½ in
2 cm	¾ in
2.5 cm	1 in
3 cm	1¼ in
4 cm	1½ in
5 cm	2 in
6 cm	2½ in
7 cm	2¾ in
8 cm	3¼ in
9 cm	3½ in
10 cm	4 in
12 cm	4½ in
15 cm	6 in
17 cm	6½ in
18 cm	7 in
20 cm	8 in
23 cm	9 in
24 cm	9½ in
25 cm	10 in
30 cm	12 in

Oven Temperatures

Celsius	Fahrenheit	Gas mark	Description
110º C	225º F	¼	cool
130º C	250º F	½	cool
140º C	275º F	1	very low
150º C	300º F	2	very low
170º C	325º F	3	low
180º C	350º F	4	moderate
190º C	375º F	5	moderate/hot
200º C	400º F	6	hot
220º C	425º F	7	hot
230º C	455º F	8	very hot

Basics

Bumbu

The simplest route to success with many dishes in Betawi cuisine, street food and regional Indonesian cuisine, is to understand the bumbu. Bumbu is basically a paste or dry mix of spices such as ginger, galangal, turmeric, aromatic ginger, with or without chillies, ground with a pestle and mortar into various coloured combinations:

White paste consists of shallots, garlic, ginger, galangal, candlenuts. Sometimes the white part of lemon grass can be added into the mixture. No chillies or turmeric are added.

Red paste is white paste plus chillies.

Yellow paste add fresh turmeric to the red paste or white paste

Green –a combination of green chillies and shallots and a touch of lime juice and baby salted fish are often added to create umami flavours.

In addition to dried spices and salt, each provincial region includes its own selection of fresh herbs, aromatic leaves or fruits to add to each paste such as lemon grass, pandan, curry, turmeric and lime leaves, kecombrang (ginger flowers), fresh belimbing wuluh (carambola), dried belimbing wuluh (known as asam sunti) dried wild mango, tamarind, tomatoes and basil, among others. In some regions, black nut (keluak) paste is added to give a strong black finish with an earthy flavour. Kecombrang (ginger flower) and andaliman (fresh green sichuan pepper) can be added to create a distinctive flavour.

Paste is fried in a wok with oil, reduced to a drier texture for meat dishes, including chicken, duck and pork as well as seafood. Vegetables can then be added and depending on the recipe some coconut milk. Other cooking techniques involve uncooked bumbu and herbs mixed into meat, fish or tofu and wrapped in banana leaves, before being steamed or barbecued. Large bamboo stems are used for steaming mixtures of paste, herbs and pork on barbeque fires. Pork is eaten where Christianity or Hindu beliefs predominate and this includes Manado in North Sulawesi, Toraja in South Sulawesi and Bali as well as among the Batak people of Sumatra. The basic bumbu paste infused with other herbs, leaves, fruits or peanuts as well as citrus, tamarind or dried fruits differentiates regional Indonesian cooking.

Sambal and Pickles

Sambal

Adding sambal to a bowl of noodles, soto soup, a plate of fried rice or barbecued fish is an essential part of Jakarta's street food culture and regional Indonesian cuisine in general. Sambal is a mixture of two or more ingredients to provide extra layers of flavour for any dish. Simple sambal consists of only two ingredients such as ground chillies and salt or chopped chillies with sweet or salty soya sauce. There are in fact hundreds of different sambals offered by Jakarta street food stalls representing regional Indonesian cuisine. Everyone has different tolerance to the fiery spiciness of specific variations. Sambal is perfect for marinating before cooking, and as a dipping sauce. I use sambal 'ijo' as a pesto sauce in a number of my modern Indonesian recipes.

Here are some varieties of sambal that you can prepare in your own kitchen.

Raw Sambal

A combination of uncooked ingredients with one or two cooked additions such as shrimp paste, terasi or belacan. You may replace the shrimp paste with one or two tablespoons of fish sauce or 1-2 pieces ground anchovies.

Bali Sambal Mata

This is a mix of raw chillies, shallots and lemongrass from Bali offering delicious multiple layers of flavor, a combination of spicy and tangy with the fragrance of the lemon grass. Add kecombrang or ginger flower if you can, for even more flavours. This sambal is also perfect as a pasta sauce or salad dressing. Shrimp paste or anchovies can be added as another option.

Serves 8
- 100gr shallots, peeled and sliced thinly
- 25gr garlic, peeled and chopped finely
- 50gr cabe rawit, red bird-eye chillies, sliced thinly
- 10gr shrimp paste or 1 tbsp, roasted, replace with 1-2 pieces of anchovies or 1-2 tbsp of fish sauce
- 10 lime leaves, with the middle rough stalks removed, and sliced finely
- 4 stalks of lemon grass, use the white part only, sliced thinly
- Juice of 3-4 limes
- 100ml coconut oil or any oil
- Salt to season

To give more layers of flavours: Add 1-2 small ginger flower buds sliced thinly

- Grind the chillies finely and set aside.
- Grind the shrimp paste finely and transfer into a medium bowl.
- Add half of the coconut oil into the ground shrimp paste and mix well.
- Add the rest of the ingredients.
- Season with salt and add the lime juice and mix well. Check the final seasoning. It should be spicy, tangy with umami flavours from the shrimp paste.
- Add sliced ginger flower for a new variety of sambal mata.

Manado and Maluku Sambal Gohu
Chilli and Basil Salsa

This sambal is a mixture of finely chopped shallots, chillies, basil and lime juice to give it a mega kick. Sprinkle with kanari, local almonds or regular almonds for extra texture and flavour. This sambal is normally served with tuna sashimi or ceviche.

Serves 4-6
- 10-15 red chillies, thinly sliced
- 100gr shallots, peeled and finely chopped
- A handful of basil, finely chopped
- 100ml lime juice
- 1 tsp salt

- Simply put all the ingredients into a bowl and mix well.
- Ready to serve with sliced fresh tuna sashimi or thin beef carpaccio.

Dabu-dabu

Normally green tomatoes are used for this salsa, but I prefer red ones.

Serves 4
- 3 red tomatoes, deseeded and diced
- 4 shallots, thinly sliced
- 2 red chillies, thinly sliced
- 2 tbsp lime juice
- 3 tbsp extra virgin olive oil
- A small handful of torn mint or basil
- Salt and black pepper to taste

- Put all ingredients in a bowl. Mix well.
- Serve immediately.

You can create another sambal with belimbing wuluh, sour finger carambola or finger lime to give extra texture and fresh taste.

Cooked Sambal

Most of the ingredients are cooked, using steaming, sautéing or boiling methods. It is essential to add some acidity (lime juice or tamarind) and salt for a delicious sambal.

Sambal *Bajak*

"Bajak" sambal is tastier than regular sambal. The texture is drier as dried chillies are used in this sambal.

Serve 200gr sambal
- 50gr dried red bird's eye chillies
- 50gr dried curly red chillies
- 100ml hot water
- 100gr shallots, peeled and thinly sliced
- 50gr cloves garlic, peeled and thinly sliced
- 10cm galangal, peeled, thinly sliced
- 4 lemon grass stalks, white part roughly chopped.
- 4 bay leaves
- 100ml tamarind water (see page 39)
- 100gr tomatoes, discard seeds.
- 1 shrimp paste, fried or grilled
- 1 tsp salt
- 1 tsp sugar
- 50ml vegetables oil

- Soak the dry chillies with hot water for 5 minutes, Set aside.
- Grind all the ingredients using a pestle and mortar or a blender, Set aside.
- Heat a large frying pan, add the oil, add the paste and cook for 15 minutes. Add the shrimp paste and cook for another 5 minutes
- Add the tamarind water, tomatoes and bay leaves and simmer for another 20 minutes.
- Season with salt and sugar, set aside to cool until ready to serve.

Green Sambal
Sambal Ijo

For the Green sambal:
- 150 grs large green chillies
- 100 grs shallots, peeled and roughly chopped
- 25 grs local basil leaves or kemangi
- 3 cloves of garlic
- 100 ml extra virgin coconut oil
- 2 tbsp roasted or deep fried dried anchovies (ikan teri Medan)
- 2 tbsp lime juice
- 2 tbsp coconut oil

- Bring to boil one litre of water.
- Add green chillies and cook for 2 minutes, then add basil and cook for 15 seconds.
- Drain and transfer chillies and basil into ice-cold water.
- Set aside for 5-7minutes then drain.
- Heat a frying pan. Add 2 tbsp olive oil, shallots and garlic. Sauté for 7 minutes in medium heat, stirring all the time.
- Add chillies, basil and olive oil.
- Process until ingredients are blended well with thick sambal texture.
- Transfer the mixture into a bowl and add lime juice and half of the dried anchovies.
- Warm this mixture and add the rest of the dried anchovies, just before serving.

Simple boiled chillies sambal
Sambal rebus

- 10 red chillies, boiled for 7 minutes
- 20 ml water
- salt to season

- Boiled the chillies for 5 minutes, remove from the boiling water, ground finely.
- Add the water and salt, mixed well and ready to serve.

Pickles

Pineapple Pickled
Pacri Nanas

This is a delightful refreshing condiment of pineapple pickled with coconut and spices, the perfect companion to duck curry, or it can be used as an amuse bouche.

Serves 10
- 1 whole pineapple. Peel and remove the eyes. Cut into large bite sizes.
- 4 large red chillies, discard seeds and chopped roughly.
- 4 star anis
- 2 sticks cinnamon
- 100gr sugar
- 100ml water
- 3 tbsp apple vinegar or white vinegar
- Salt
- 200ml coconut milk

- Rinse the pineapple with cold water and cut into bite sized portions. Sprinkle with sea salt. Set aside.
- To make the spiced sugar syrup, put sugar, water, chillies and star anis in a medium pan and bring to the boil. Reduce the liquid one third.
- Add the coconut, pineapple, vinegar and season with salt. Taste the final seasoning and cook for another 5 minutes.
- Transfer the mixture into a bowl and set aside to cool. Ready to serve hot with duck curry or as an amuse bouche.

Pickled Shallots
Acar Bawang Merah

Often served with martabak, fried noodles or nasi goreng this sambal provides extra flavour and a touch of acidity. For variety you may replace the shallots with whole birds-eye chillies or cucumber or you can mix them together.

- 250gr shallots, peeled
- 400ml water
- 100ml white vinegar (apple vinegar or rice vinegar)
- 1 tbsp of salt

- Place the whole shallots in a large bowl.
- In a large saucepan combine the water, vinegar and salt and bring to the boil. Add the shallots. Turn the heat off and let the mixture cool before transferring into sterilized jars.
- You may keep the pickles at room temperature for 2-3 days or in the refrigerator for up to 10 days.

Yellow Pickles
Acar Kuning

This yellow pickle has a distinctive curry flavour with the yellow from the fresh turmeric roots. It is very versatile, complementing steamed fish, chicken or any protein.

Makes 300gr pickles for 2-3 jars
- 100gr carrots, peeled cut into strips
- 100gr cauliflower florets
- 100gr cucumbers, seeded, cut into ½ cm half rounds.
- 50gr large red chillies

For the Paste:
- 50gr shallots
- 4 cloves of garlic
- 2 candlenuts
- 5gr fresh turmeric, roasted or 1 tsp turmeric powder
- ½ tsp white pepper

Other Ingredients:
- 10gr fresh ginger, peeled and finely grated
- 2 lemon grass stalks, crushed
- 500ml water
- 2 tbsp sugar
- 50ml white vinegar
- 2 tbsp cooking oil

- Prepare the paste first. Simply grind the ingredients finely.
- Heat the oil in the frying pan and add the paste. Cook for around 5-7 minutes. Stirring from time to time.
- Add all the vegetables. Add the lemon grass and mix well.
- Add salt, sugar and water and cook for around 2-3 minutes.
- Turn the heat off and add the vinegar and season with salt.
- Check the final seasoning and set aside to cool. Ready to transfer into sterilized jars.

Crunchy Fried Shallots
Bawang Goreng

This is a very traditional way to add an Indonesian provincial flavour to many dishes.

- 100g shallots, peeled and thinly sliced
- 1 tsp salt
- 200ml vegetable oil

- Season the shallots with salt. Heat a pan and add the oil.
- Deep fry half of the shallots until golden brown.
- Turn the heat to low. Pat the cooked shallots with a piece of kitchen towel to absorb the excess oil.
- Repeat the cooking process for the other half of the shallots.

Vegetable/Beef Stock
Kaldu Sayur/Daging

Makes 1 litre
- 2 medium carrots, washed, brushed and roughly chopped
- 2 spring onions, washed and roughly chopped
- 4 cloves of garlic
- Small bunch of celery leaves
- 1¼ litres cold water

- Put all ingredients in a pan, bring to the boil and cook for 20 minutes on a low heat.
- Bring the water to the boil and simmer for 20 minutes on low heat.
- Remove from heat and leave to settle for about 10 minutes.
- Strain the liquid and the stock is ready.

Tips: For fish stock, sauté all the vegetables from the vegetable stock with 2 tbsp oil for about 5 minutes, add 2 litres water and ½kg raw fish bones and fish head. Bring to the boil, skimming the scum off the surface with a wide spoon. Follow the remaining steps of the cooking method above.

Roasted Sweet Potatoes
Ubi Merah Panggang

Sweet potatoes are available widely throughout Indonesia. They have different colours: orange, purple and white. This is basically a version of roasted potato. Any colour will be suitable.

Serves 4-6
- 1kg sweet potatoes, peeled and cut into big cubes
- 1½ litres water
- 1 tsp salt
- 2 tbsp vegetable oil

- Pre-heat the oven to 180°C or gas mark 4.
- Bring the water to the boil. Add the potatoes and cook for around 15 minutes until half done.
- 5 minutes before the potatoes are ready, spread the oil onto a baking tray and place in the oven.
- Strain the potatoes and set aside. Remove the hot tray from the oven and set the potatoes on the tray.
- Sprinkle with salt and return to the oven. Cook for 30-40 minutes until soft. Serve hot.

Tamarind Water
Air Asam Jawa

Makes 100ml
- 50g tamarind pulp
- 125ml hot water

- Put the tamarind pulp and the water into a bowl and leave to soften for 10 minutes.
- Break the pulp with a spoon and strain.

Palm Sugar Syrup
Sirup Gula Aren

Natural palm sugar has a beautiful fragrance and is a wonderful alternative to honey or maple syrup.

Makes 500ml
- 600g palm sugar blocks, roughly chopped
- 500ml water
- 2 pandan leaves, washed and roughly chopped

- Put all ingredients in a pan and bring to the boil on a low heat until the sugar blocks have dissolved. Simmer for 5-7 minutes.
- Leave to cool then strain.

Tips: At first, you will find the texture of the syrup is runny. It will thicken when left at room temperature. You can keep the syrup in your refrigerator for a couple weeks. If thick, the syrup will harden at room temperature. To obtain a thicker palm sugar syrup, just simmer the syrup for an extra 5 minutes.

Sugar Syrup
Sirup Gula

It is very handy to have this always in your refrigerator.

Makes 500ml
- 400g sugar
- 200ml water

- Put sugar and water into a pan and bring to simmer until all the sugar is dissolved.
- Set aside to cool until ready to use.

Pandan Extract
Sari Daun Pandan

Pandan is a natural green colouring agent and gives a wonderful fragrance to rice or palm sugar. It used throughout Indonesia.

Makes 50ml
- 4 pandan leaves, finely chopped
- 100ml water

Place the pandan leaves with water in a blender. Blend for around 1 minute or until you achieve a fine mixture. Strain.

Betawi Cuisine

Starters

Mixed vegetable wedding salad

RUJAK PENGANTIN

Associated with the special occasion of a wedding, this delicious salad is a combination of fruit and vegetables. It has sour, spicy and umami flavours from dried prawn. Use only half of a whole pineapple and you may use the rest for juicing. You may replace the fresh pineapple with tinned pineapple.

Serves 4-6

Ingredients:
- ½ whole pineapple, peeled with the 'eyes' and the rough stalk in the middle removed or 300gr tinned pineapple. Discard the syrup and rinse under cold water
- 50gr beansprouts with roots removed
- 50gr Romaine salad leaves
- 100gr white cabbage, sliced thinly
- 50gr cucumber chopped roughly with seeds removed
- 100gr firm tofu, cut into 1cm x 1cm cubes (optional)
- 3 boiled eggs (optional)
- 2 large peeled potatoes
- 50gr roasted peanuts, crushed roughly

For the Sauce:
- 150gr roasted peanuts or cashew
- 1 tbsp dried prawn, roasted and finely ground
- 2 cloves of garlic, peeled and finely grated
- 4 red chillies
- 1 tsp sugar
- 50ml rice vinegar or apple vinegar
- 200ml water
- 1-2 tbsp palm or brown sugar
- Salt to taste

Directions:
- Cut the potatoes into 1cm cube and steam until soft. Refresh with ice water to arrest the cooking process. Strain and set aside.
- Boil the eggs in room temperature water for 6 minutes to ensure a soft but firm yolk. Place eggs in ice water to arrest the cooking process.
- To prepare the sauce, finely grind the garlic, chillies and peanuts using a pestle and mortar or a blender.
- Transfer the mixture into a large pan, add water, ground roasted dried prawn and bring to the boil. Simmer for 10 minutes.
- Add the vinegar, sugar and season with salt. Check the final seasonings. Set aside to cool.
- If using eggs, peel the egg shell and slice the eggs in half.
- To serve, arrange all the salad ingredients on six serving plates or bowls. You can also serve on individual plates or bowls by dividing the salad ingredients into 6 portions. Drizzle the sauce on top of the salad, add one sliced egg and sprinkle with crushed peanuts. Serve immediately.

Tropical fruit salad served with sweet, spicy and tangy tamarind and palm sugar dressing

RUJAK BUAH

Arguably the most well-known Jakarta street food, rujak is eaten throughout the day. It's a nice touch to use a vegetable peeler to create a different texture for this humble dish of cut fruit. The tamarind is key, introducing a delicious tang. Rujak is adaptable, from barbecue party to fine dinner. The texture of the sauce resembles honey. You can substitute apple, red onion, iceberg salad leaves, cucumber and carrot if the tropical fruits in the recipe are not available. Sometimes ground peanuts are added to the dish.

Serves 4-6

Ingredients:

For the Rujak:
- 3 water apples, washed and cut into small cubes
- 1 small pineapple, peeled and cut into small cubes
- 1 unripe mango, peeled and finely grated using a julienne slicer
- 2 segments of pomelo, broken into small pieces
- 1 small green papaya with orange flesh. Use a vegetable peeler to create ribbons of papaya. Roll each of them
- 2 medium ripe star fruit, sliced a half-centimeter thick.

For the Sauce:
- 2-3 red birdseye chillies (giving a spicier taste) blanched
- 50 gr palm sugar block, chopped finely or replaced with brown sugar
- Half tbsp of good quality dried shrimp (roasted and ground) or alternatively 2 tbsp fish sauce
- 2 tbsp tamarind paste (around 50 gr)
- 150ml water
- 100gr roasted peanuts, roughly ground (optional)
- Salt to taste

Directions:
- To make the sauce, grind the chillies, shrimp paste, palm sugar (or brown sugar) until smooth. Transfer the mixture into a medium bowl.
- Mix water and tamarind paste and squeeze with your hand. Mix well, strain and set aside.
- Add the ground shrimp and tamarind water into the sauce mixture. Mix well and aim for a honey consistency. Add a touch of salt and check the final seasoning.
- Prepare all the fruit and set aside.
- To serve, arrange each fruit in the middle of 4 serving plates. Add dots of sauce around the fruit. Serve extra sauce in a small glass container and sprinkle some roasted peanut over the fruits if you wish. Serve immediately.

Mixed vegetables and fruits served with a spicy, sour and sweet sauce

ASINAN JAKARTA

This is a very refreshing and colourful salad dish with sweet, spicy and tangy flavours from vinegar. It can be served with rice or shrimp crackers. A nice touch is to use a vegetable peeler to create a short spaghetti texture for this humble dish of julienned fruit. I serve it in a martini glass to give a modern touch. It is a perfect starter for any occasion.

Serves 4-6

Ingredients:
For the Salad:
- 2 medium carrots, peeled and grated
- 2 medium cucumbers, seeds removed and cut into small cubes
- One quarter of a white cabbage (about 100 gr), shredded
- 50gr bean sprouts, rinsed, dried with roots removed
- 150gr white firm tofu, boil (optional)
- 100gr jicama, peeled and grated
- 100gr pineapple, cut into small cubes
- 50gr roasted peanuts or cashew, roughly chopped (optional)

For the Dressing:
- 3 red large papaya chillies, seeds discarded
- 2-3 red birds-eye chillies boiled for 5 minutes and dunked in cold water
- 50ml tbsp vinegar
- 150ml simple sugar syrup
- 2 tbsp dried shrimp, roasted and ground finely
- Salt to taste

Directions:
- To roast the peanuts: Pre-heat oven to 150°C. Place the peanuts on a baking tray and cook for 10 minutes or until golden brown. Alternatively cook in a dry frying pan over low heat for 5-7 minutes until golden brown, stirring constantly. Set aside to cool.
- To make the sauce: boil all chillies for around 10 minutes. Remove the seeds of the papaya chillies but retain the seeds of the birds eye chillies. The large papaya chillies give a vivid red coloured sauce and also act as thickening agent.
- Put the sugar syrup and chillies into a blender and run until smooth. Strain the liquid over a bowl.
- Add the vinegar and add a touch of salt. Taste the final seasoning and add more sugar syrup if necessary.
- To serve, place the mixed vegetables and fruits into 4 or 6 martini glasses. Add the sauce. Sprinkle the roughly ground nuts and serve immediately.

Mixed vegetable salad, tofu, potatoes and tempeh

GADO-GADO

This is one of my favourite vegetarian dishes. It is easy to make and full of flavour. Although originally gado-gado is from Batavia or Jakarta, it is available all over Indonesia as a national dish. The recipe provides the classic gado-gado taste, but with lighter flavours. The lightness is achieved through dry roasting, not deep-frying the peanuts as in the traditional way. You may also use peanut butter for this recipe but to make this meal 100% vegetarian do not add shrimp paste or fish sauce.

Serves 4

- 30gr amaranth leaves, replaced with young spinach
- 50gr white or red cabbage
- 2 small chayote, peeled and cut into wedges
- 30gr bean sprouts, roots removed
- 1 medium bitter melon, cut into 8 round pieces with seeds removed (optional)

- 50gr long beans or French beans, cut into 1cm lengths
- 1 corn on the cob, sliced to remove the corn or replace with 100gr tinned corn
- 2 soft boiled eggs
- 50gr fried tempe, soya cake (optional)
- 100gr tofu, cut into cubes and fried (optional)
- 2 medium carrots, sliced with vegetable peeler or julienne peeler
- 2-3 tbsp deep-fried shallots (optional)

For Peanut Sauce:

- 50gr palm sugar block
- 100ml tamarind water (that's 50gr tamarind paste diluted with 150 ml hot water)
- Half tsp roasted shrimp paste
- 2-3 red birdseye chillies, sliced thinly
- 50gr roasted peanuts and 50gr roasted cashews, ground finely or 4 tbsp crunchy peanut butter
- Salt to taste

Directions:

For the Sauce:

- To roast the peanuts: place the peanuts on a baking tray and roast until golden brown at 180°C or dry roast using a frying pan for about 10 minutes or until golden and set aside to cool.
- Put all the peanuts and cashews into a strong blender and blend for few minutes or until you get a nice smooth texture with some chunky pieces.
- Transfer the peanut paste into a large bowl and add the tamarind water, sugar and ground chillies. Mix well and check the final seasoning. Add a touch of salt if necessary. Set aside.
- To prepare the eggs: place the eggs in room temperature water in a medium sized pan, bring to the boil and cook for 4-5 minutes after water has boiled. Transfer the egg into a bowl of ice water to arrest the cooking process. Remove the shell and cut into halves just before serving.

To Prepare the Vegetables:

- Steam the chayote, bitter melon and long beans or French beans. Steam the chayote first for 4 minutes, add the sliced bitter melon and steam for 4 minutes and the long beans for 4 minutes. Refresh all the vegetables in iced water for 2-3 minutes to preserve a vivid green and to arrest the cooking process. Strain all the vegetables.
- To serve: mix all the vegetables well and divide into 4 individual salad plates. Add the fried tempe and tofu (if used) and drizzle with peanut sauce. Place 2 sliced of soft-boiled egg on top and sprinkle with deep-fried shallots. Put some extra sauce in small bowls for the table if necessary. Serve immediately.

Ketoprak with griddled chicken breast

KETOPRAK DENGAN IRISAN DADA AYAM

This classic dish is a mixture of compressed rice and rice noodles, served with a touch of fried tofu and sliced cabbage. It has distinctive raw garlic flavours with a delicious tangy peanut sauce and a drizzle of sweet soya sauce. This is a great dish to prepare a couple hours in advance and in the refrigerator until required. For best results the hot-griddled chicken should be cooked at the last minute before serving. Also I added grated carrots and lemon basil for that extra layer of flavour and colour.

Serves 4-6

Ingredients:
- 150gr rice noodles
- 2 medium carrots, peeled and grated
- 100gr bean sprouts, roots removed
- 1 large cucumber, seeds discarded and chopped into half cm slices
- Small bunch of basil, leaves only
- 100gr firm tofu
- 3 soft boiled eggs

For the Chicken:
- 4 skinless chicken breasts
- juice of 1 lime, salt and black pepper for seasoning
- 2 tbsp coconut oil or vegetable oil

For the Sauce:
- 200gr roasted peanuts (or cashews)
- 2 cloves peeled garlic, ground finely
- 3-4 red birds eye chillies, sliced thinly
- 2-3 tbsp palm sugar
- 1-2 tbsp sweet soya sauce
- 150ml tamarind water
- Salt to taste

Directions:
- First prepare the sauce. Roast the peanut in the pre-heated 180°C oven or in a dry frying pan for around 15 minutes or until golden brown. Stir from time to time and set aside to cool.
- Put all the sauce ingredients into a strong blender and blend for 30 seconds. You may choose to grind peanuts and cashews roughly to give a nice texture to the sauce. If you prefer to have a creamy texture blend for over one minute. To achieve the texture of runny honey, simply add more tamarind water. Transfer the sauce into a bowl and set aside.
- Cut the tofu into bite sizes, boil for 5 minutes and set aside to cool.
- Season the chicken breasts with lime juice, salt and a drizzle of coconut oil or vegetable oil. Add black pepper one minute before the cooking time is finished. Set aside.
- Heat a griddle pan until very hot, place the chicken and cook for around 3-4 minutes on each side. Turn the heat off and cover the pan. The chicken will continue to cook but the meat will not dry out.
- To prepare the rice noodles, simply follow the instructions on the packet. Normally cooking time is around 2 minutes. After boiling put the noodles into ice water to arrest the cooking process, drain and set aside to cool.
- To serve: mix the rice noodles and all the vegetables and herbs either in one large serving dish or individual dishes. Drizzle with plenty of peanut sauce and toss well. Slice the chicken and place on top of the salad mixture. Or you can also serve the sauce in small individual bowls as an alternative.

Vegetable curry, soft boiled egg with rice cake

KETUPAT SAYUR

This is a comfort food for Jakartans, either for breakfast, lunch or dinner. The dried chillies give a kind of reddish colour to the broth and the dried shrimp and shrimp paste give amazing umami flavour. Ketupat means rice cooked inside young coconut leaves. To make it simpler, I use lontong, which is compressed rice boiled in bags.

Serves 4-6

Ingredients:
- 1 large chayote, peeled and cut into match sticks
- 100gr long beans or French beans, cut into 3cm lengths
- 100gr carrots, peeled and cut into ½cm pieces
- 6 soft boiled eggs
- 100gr white firm tofu
- 3 salam leaves or bay leaves
- 2 lemon grass leaves, crushed and tied into a knot
- 1 litre water
- 500ml coconut cream
- 1 tsp sugar

- 1 tbsp good quality dried prawn, soaked in hot water and ground finely
- 2 tbsp coconut oil or vegetable oil
- Salt and black pepper to taste

For the Paste:
- 50gr shallots
- 3 cloves of garlic
- 3 bird eye chillies
- 3 red curly dried chillies
- 10gr each fresh ginger or galangal or replaced with 1 tsp each of ginger or galangal powder
- 5gr fresh turmeric, roasted or ½ tsp turmeric powder

- 1 tsp shrimp paste or 2 tbsp fish sauce

For the Compressed Rice:
- 1 boil-a-bag 20cm x 30cm
- 100gr jasmine rice
- 400ml water for adding to the rice boil-in-the-bag
- 2 litres water for boiling
- 1 tsp of sea salt

Other Ingredients:
- 50gr shrimp crackers (optional)
- 3 tbsp crunchy deep-fried shallots

Directions:
- To prepare the compressed rice: fill a large saucepan two-thirds full of room temperature water. Add 1 tsp of salt and bring to the boil. Rinse the rice and put inside the bag and add 400ml water. Tie the top of the plastic with string. Put the boil in-the bag rice, into the pot and continue boiling for 90 minutes. Add more hot water if necessary, with boiling water from a kettle, so that the rice remains covered al the time.
- At the end of 90 minutes, remove the bag and put on a flat plate. Leave to cool completely. The lontong will be at their best after they have been refrigerated for at least 3 hours or ideally overnight. Remove from the refrigerator 1 hour before use.
- Finely grind all the paste ingredients either with pestle or mortar or strong blender (except the fish sauces if you use it). Heat a large sauce pan, add 2 tbsp coconut oil or any vegetable oil and sauté the paste for around 3-5 minutes until fragrant. Stir continuously.
- Add water and salam leaves, lemon grass, chayote, carrots and bring to the boil. Cook the chayote until soft (around 5-7 minutes). Season with salt and black pepper.

- Add the long beans, tofu, sugar and cook for 5 mintues. Add the coconut milk and bring to a simmer. Check the final seasoning. You will have a creamy coconut broth with soft vegetables.
- To serve: Cut the other end of the compressed rice and discard the bag. Cut the compressed rice into chunks or wedges (bite sizes about 2cm thick) using a large sharp knife moistened with water. Place on a plate or bowl suitable for the microwave. Reheat the compressed rice for 2-3 minutes in the microwave.
- Place 4-5 pieces of compressed rice in 6 individual serving bowls and add the vegetable curry with enough vegetables, tofu pieces and broth. Sprinkle with crunchy fried shallots and top with sliced soft boiled eggs. Serve hot immediately.

Betawi Omelette with ginger and turmeric broth

KERAK TELUR ALA MODERN DENGAN KUAH JAHE DAN KUNYIT

Kerak telur is a signature Betawi dish enjoyed as a snack with dried coconut. I really like the idea to serve this dish as a delicious and elegant starter for a memorable dinner party. It combines the flavours of dried coconut with mixed spices. I gently roast the coconut to retain as much of its natural moisture as possible.

Serves 4

For the Omelette:
- 4 whole eggs
- 4 tbsp serundeng (spiced roasted coconut, see recipe below)
- 50gr beansprouts, roots removed
- 1 tbsp deep-fried shallots
- Small bunch celery leaves, chopped finely
- 2 tbsp coconut oil or vegetable oil
- Salt to taste

For the Ginger broth:
- 600ml water
- 50gr fresh ginger
- 30gr fresh turmeric; sliced thinly
- Season with freshly ground white pepper and salt

**For the Serundeng,
Spiced Roasted Coconut:**
- 150gr or a quarter of a whole coconut. Remove the skin and grate finely. Alternatively, use 100gr-desiccated coconut
- 10gr each of fresh ginger, galangal and turmeric, finely grated
- 1 tsp flaked chilli
- 2 tbsp good quality small dried prawns, roasted and ground finely
- 2-3 tbsp deep-fried shallots, ground roughly

Directions:
- To make the ginger broth, put the water in a medium pot, add the ginger, bring to the boil and simmer for 30 minutes to infuse. Season with a touch of salt and white pepper. Set aside.
- In the meantime, make the spiced roasted coconut. Use a dry heated frying pan. Add and stir the spices and coconut for an even mix. Roast for around 30 minutes until slightly golden brown. Add the ground dried prawn and fried shallots. Mix well. Set aside to cool.
- To make the omelette mixture, crack one or two eggs, add 1 or 2 tbsp of roasted coconut and spices, beat gently and set aside.
- Place a small frying pan over a medium heat and add a half-tbsp coconut oil or vegetable oil for each individual omelette. Pour the egg mixture into the pan. Tilt the pan and cook the omelette in the lower half. This will give the omelette a crescent-moon shape. Keep folding the egg mixture for 1-2 minutes until it has set.
- Roll the omelette sideways to cook the reverse side. Cook for another 30 seconds. Repeat the process to make a further 3 portions. Transfer the cooked omelettes into a baking dish in the oven at 150°C.
- To serve, place each omelette in the middle of individual serving dishes. Add the warm broth. Add the raw beansprouts, sprinkle with chopped parsley and crunchy shallots and serve warm.

Mixed vegetables with young tamarind broth

SAYUR ASEM

This is so refreshingly delicious for vegetarians. Don't worry if you do not have jack fruit and melinjo leaves. You may change the vegetables with young spinach, carrots, French beans and cauliflower. You may also use tamarind paste or ripe tamarind but the broth will turn a darker brown.

Serves 4

Ingredients
For the Broth:
- 3 young tamarind pods, broken into halves or 50gr tamarind paste
- 50g shallots, peeled and thinly sliced
- 2 cloves of garlic (optional), peeled and sliced thinly, 3 red chilli peppers, ground finely
- 5cm fresh galangal, thinly sliced
- ½ tsp shrimp paste, roasted and ground finely or 1 tsp fish sauce
- 3 candlenuts, ground finely (macadamia nuts are a good substitute)
- 1 litre water
- 1 tbsp sugar
- Salt

Vegetables:
- 50gr fresh melinjo nuts or peanuts
- 100gr fresh corn kernels sliced from 2 medium cobs or replaced with tinned corn
- one medium chayote, peeled under running water
- 150gr each of young jackfruit, pumpkin and green raw papaya, peeled and chopped into cubes
- 50gr small bunch of melinjo leaves or young spinach
- 50gr long beans or French beans

Directions:
- Put one litre water into a large pan and add fresh melinjo nuts. Then add a ground chillies, candlenuts, shrimp paste. Add sliced galangal, shallots, garlic and young tamarind pods and bring to the boil. Simmer for 30-40 minutes to infuse the flavors and to soften the melinjo nuts. Season with salt and add palm sugar.
- Strain the broth into a different pan and add the jackfruit first and cook for 10 minutes. Then add the rest of the vegetables except the melinjo leaves and corn and cook for another 10 minutes or until soft.
- In the meantime, remove the skins from the melinjo nuts and set aside. Also remove the shell and thin skin from the melinjo nuts.
- Before serving, check seasoning and add the corn, melinjo skins, nuts and melinjo leaves and cook for 3 minutes.
- Ladle the soup into four individual soup bowls and serve hot immediately.

Soto

Soto is an Indonesian soup or stew mostly found in Java and most popularly prepared using beef or chicken. There are many varieties found outside of Java including East Kalimantan, Banjarmasin and South Sulawesi, Soto Makassar, Soto Padang, West Sumatera. Depending on local custom, the dish is described as coto, soto or sroto. The main differences lie in the spices, herbs and fragrant ingredients used with or without coconut.

Soto, Soup,
Laksa and Rice

Soto Betawi with a twist

SOTO BETAWI

Soto Betawi is a creamy beef soup that consists of a beef broth enriched with coconut milk and a combination of herbs and spices. Unlike the clear or transparent broth of other 'sotos', the Betawi version is thicker and has a distinct light curry-like flavour. For the adventurous this version of soto can also be served with kidney, tripe or liver boiled and deep-fried, sliced and served with the beef milk or coconut broth. This recipe is lighter with the beef stewed slowly until tender, the spices and herbs added together with the coconut cream just before serving. Traditionally, all soto is served with a bowl of rice but I think it is delicious to enjoy as is. You can experience Soto Tangkar by simply adding sweet soya sauce into the soup.

Serves 6-8

Ingredients:
- 800gr quality stewing beef or beef skirt cut into 2cm pieces
- 500 ml coconut cream
- 1.5 litres of beef stock
- 2-3 tbsp coconut oil or vegetable oil
- Salt and black pepper to taste

For the Paste:
- 75gr shallots
- 4 cloves of garlic
- 4 roasted candlenuts
- 1 tbsp roasted whole coriander seeds

Other Ingredients:
- 1 tsp of freshly grated nutmeg
- 3 lime leaves

Extra Ingredients:
- Small bunch of celery leaves or Chinese parsley
- 1 finely chopped spring onion
- 3 large ripe tomatoes cut into small cubes
- Juice of 2 limes
- Crunchy fried shallots (optional)
- 5 red birds eye chillies, ground finely

Directions:
- Prepare the paste: put all the ingredients into a mortar and grind finely with a pestle. Set aside.
- Season the beef with salt and black pepper.
- Heat a large pot and add 2 tbsp of coconut oil or vegetable oil and the beef to brown in batches. You may add a little bit more oil if the mixture is too dry. Set beef aside.
- In the same pot add the paste and cook for 4-5 minutes or until fragrant.
- Return the beef pieces, mix well and cook for around a minute, stirring all the time.
- Add the beef stock, lime leaves and grated nutmeg. Simmer for 1.5 hours to 2 hours until the meat is tender. Season with salt.
- Add the coconut milk to the mixture.
- Add lime juice and check the seasoning. Add more salt if necessary.
- Divide the soto into 6 to 8 serving bowls and garnish with chopped tomatoes, Chinese parsley, spring onions and fried shallots. Serve the ground fresh chillies and sliced lime leaves on the side. Serve hot immediately.

Jakarta noodles soto

SOTO MIE JAKARTA

This beef noodle soup is distinctive for its fragrant broth. You can choose a vegetarian option using vegetable spring rolls in place of meat. There are plenty of different textures and delicious fragrances in this soto.

Serves 4

- 300gr goulash meat (beef shank)
- 2 tbsp coconut oil or vegetable oil
- 1 litre beef stock
- 200gr fresh egg noodles or any dried noodles. Follow cooking instructions on package
- 100gr white or red cabbage, sliced thinly lengthwise
- 2 red tomatoes, de-seeded and cut into small cubes
- 4 medium vegetarian, chicken or prawn spring rolls
- 2 tbsp fried shallots

To Make the Paste:
- 50gr shallots, peeled and chopped roughly
- 3 cloves of garlic, peeled and chopped roughly
- 3 red curly chillies, chopped roughly
- 3cm each fresh galangal and ginger, peeled and chopped roughly or replace with 1 tsp ginger and galangal powder

Other Ingredients:
- 5 lime leaves, each torn into 2-3 pieces
- 2 bay leaves
- 2 spring onions, chopped finely
- 2 lemon grass sticks, crushed
- Juice of 2 limes

Directions:
- Grind finely all the ingredients for the paste. Set aside
- Heat a large pan, add coconut oil or vegetable oil and the paste and sauté for around 3-4 minutes. Add the beef. Mix well and cook for a further 2-3 minutes and add water or beef stock, all the extra ingredients except the lime juice and simmer until the beef is very soft.
- Season the stock with salt and black pepper. Add the lime juice. Check the final seasoning,
- Boil 1 litre water. Add the noodles and cook for 2 minutes. Drain or follow cooking intstructions on package to soften dried noodles.
- Prepare the spring rolls and make sure it is ready and hot.
- To serve: Put the noodles in 4-6 individual bowls or one large serving bowl and add sliced cabbage on top, together with cubed tomatoes and chopped flat parsley. Add the thinly sliced beef and sliced spring rolls.
- Sprinkle with crunchy shallots and serve hot immediately.

Goat, carrot and potato soup

SUP KAMBING

A street food favourite and a bowl of comfort, this recipe reflects the influence of the Middle East. You may replace the goat with lamb.

Serves 4-6

- 600gr goat or lamb stewing meat , cut into 2cm pieces
- 2 litres goat/lamb/vegetable stock
- 2 tbsp coconut oil or vegetable oil
- 3 large carrots, peeled and cut into 1cm pieces
- 3 large potatoes, peeled and cut into 1cm pieces
- 2 sticks celery, peeled and cut into 1cm pieces
- 6 tomatoes, deseeded and chopped into medium cubes
- 2 tbsp crunchy fried shallots

Sliced or Chopped Finely:
- 10cm fresh ginger
- 75 gr shallots
- 4 cloves of garlic
- 4 red birdseye chillies

Other Ingredients:
- 8 whole cloves, roasted and finely ground
- 1 stick of cinnamon
- 1 tsp of freshly grated nutmeg

Directions:
- Season the meat with salt and black pepper.
- Heat a large pot, add coconut oil or vegetable oil and brown the meat. Set aside.
- Using the same pan, add the sliced or chopped ingredients and sauté for 2-3 minutes. Add the cloves, cinnamon and nutmeg. Mix well.
- Add the goat or lamb meat and the stock. Simmer for 2 to 2 ½ hours or until tender.
- In the middle of the cooking process, add the cut potatoes, carrot, celery and half of the tomatoes and continue simmering the mixture until the meat and the vegetables are tender but still whole.
- Add the rest of the tomatoes and cook for an extra 5 minutes. Check the final seasoning.
- Divide the soup into 4 or 6 individual bowls or one serving bowl. Sprinkle with finely sliced Chinese parsley and crunchy shallots. Serve immediately.

Oxtail soup

SUP BUNTUT

An easy to make rustic recipe but it does take time. You can promote it into a fine dining offering by converting the broth into oxtail consommé, removing the oxtail meat from the bone and using it to make delicious dumplings, add roasted slices of tenderloin beef and serve with the same vegetables and herbs as in the classic oxtail soup.

Serves 6-8

- 1.5kg chopped oxtail, fat trimmed and discarded
- 100gr gr shallots, peeled and sliced thinly
- 3 cloves of garlic peeled, finely minced
- 5cm each of fresh ginger and galangal, peeled and finely grated
- 2 spring onions, roughly chopped
- 4 carrots, peeled and chopped around 1cm length
- 2 large potatoes, cut into medium cubes
- 2 stick cinnamon
- 1 tsp whole cloves
- 7 whole nutmeg, roughly cracked
- 1 tsp whole black pepper

- 5 lime leaves
- 2½ litres beef or vegetables stock (see page 38)
- Juice of 2 limes
- 1 tbsp roughly chopped Chinese parsley
- Salt and black pepper to season

Other Ingredients:

- 2 tbsp crunchy deep fried shallots
- 2 tbsp finely chopped Chinese parsley
- 2 tbsp finely chopped spring onions
- 2 tomatoes deseeded and chopped in small squares
- Extra pieces of sliced lime and sliced chillies (optional)

Directions:

- Place the oxtail into a large pot, cover with room temperature water and bring to the boil. After boiling for 3 minutes, discard the water and rinse the oxtail. Add more room temperature water to cover the oxtail, bring to boil again. On the 3rd and last time, add 2½ litres beef stock or water to cover the oxtail and add the ingredients and spices except the carrots and potatoes. Simmer for 3-4 hours. If the stock starts to boil away, top up, so that the oxtail is always covered with water.
- Add the carrots and potatoes after 3 hours cooking the oxtail. Cook and simmer together for another 30 minutes or until tender and soft.
- Season the mixture with salt and add lime juice. Now, you have a delicious soup with tender oxtail, whole shallots, soft vegetables.
- To serve: arrange two pieces of oxtail and some vegetables on four individual large bowls. Add the liquid of the soup accordingly and add chopped raw tomatoes on top. Sprinkle with crunchy shallots, chopped Chinese parsley, and the thinly sliced red birds eye chillies. Serve immediately.

Prawn laksa

LAKSA

Laksa is a spicy coconut soup with rice noodles and prawns. It is a traditional dish in the Bogor area. The similarity with Singaporean laksa or Malaysian laksa shows how much Indonesia, Malaysia and Singapore share the peranakan cuisine, named after Chinese migrants who introduced their cuisine into the region.

Ingredients:
- 400gr thick rice vermicelli (parboiled and drained dry)
- 50gr dried prawns (washed and ground),
- 200gr bean sprouts (washed with water)
- 250ml coconut cream
- 500ml prawn stock
- 3 limes (sliced)
- 3 lime leaves
- 2 tsps sugar
- salt to taste

For the Paste:
- 2 stalks lemon grass (roughly slice the white only)
- 5gr galangal and turmeric (roughly sliced)
- 4 candlenuts
- 10 red dried chillies (soak in warm water and drain)
- 50gr shallots
- 1-tbsp coriander powder
- 1 tsps shrimp paste or 2 tbsp fish sauce
- Grind all the ingredients with a blender or pestle and mortar

For the Sambal:
- 15 dried chillies (ground)
- 2 tbsp oil
- ½ tsp sugar
- salt to taste.

Other Ingredients:
- 200 gr medium sized prawns. Clean and boil in 1 litre water for 5 minutes. Remove prawns from liquid. Set aside to cool. Retain the liquid. Shell prawns, return shells to liquid and boil 10 minutes for prawn stock. Strain and set aside.
- 1 small cucumber (skin, halve, remove seeds and slice thinly)
- bunch of laksa leaves. You can find these at a traditional market, or they can be replaced with mint or coriander.

Directions:
- To make the sambal, heat oil in a wok or saucepan, lower heat, add ground chillies and cook for 5-7 minutes. Add salt and sugar.
- Remove from heat and set aside for 5 minutes.
- Transfer to a small bowl. This serves as a side dish to the laksa.
- To prepare the soup, reheat the wok or saucepan. Add 1 tbsp of oil and the paste. Cook until fragrant on low to medium heat
- Add ground dried prawns and cook for 2-3 minutes.
- Add 1 tbsp of water if the mixture is too dry.
- Add prawn stock, lime leaves and coconut milk and bring to a boil.
- Simmer for 10 minutes, stirring constantly.
- Add cooked prawns and cook for another 5 minutes. Add salt to taste.

To Serve:
- Apportion the rice vermicelli and bean sprouts into individual bowls.
- Add three or four prawns and sliced cucumber to each.
- Pour the hot soup over and sprinkle with laksa leaves.
- Serve with the sambal and sliced lime for those who like a spicier, tangy flavor.

Fragrant rice with spicy coconut dressing

NASI ULAM

This is my new interpretation of Nasi Ulam, traditionally served for breakfast. Nasi Ulam is different from Nasi Uduk or Nasi Lemak (in Malaysia) as there is no addition of coconut milk to cook the rice. Instead the coconut is freshly grated, roasted and mixed with herbs and spices. The classic method is to serve plenty of rice accompanied by a small portion of protein but I have changed the composition in favour of protein rather than carbohydrates to produce a lighter meal. It is also perfect as a salad dish. I also substituted brown rice (or wild rice) for regular white rice, but that's a personal preference. Another option is to serve it with sliced griddled chicken.

Serves 4-6

- 200gr brown rice
- 250ml water
- 2 pandan leaves, chopped roughly
- 2 salam or bay leaves
- 3gr each fresh ginger and galangal, peeled and grated
- 1 lemon grass stalk, crushed and tied into a knot

Desiccated Coconut Dressing:
- 2 birds eye chillies, sliced thinly
- 30gr or 4 shallots, peeled and sliced thinly
- 1 tsp coriander seeds, roasted and ground finely
- ¼ tsp cumin seeds, roasted and ground finely
- ½ tsps shrimp paste, roasted (optional)
- 1 lemon grass stalk, use the white part only and slice thinly
- 1 tsp palm sugar
- Salt to season
- 100gr desiccated coconut
- 2 tbsp of coconut oil or vegetable oil

Other Ingredients:
- 4-6 organic boiled eggs
- 3 medium cucumbers with the seeds removed, then cut into small squares
- 18 red cherry tomatoes cut into halves
- Small bunch of kemangi or basil (leaves only)
- 50gr bean sprouts, roots removed
- 2 tbsp of crunchy fried shallots
- 2 tbsp roasted cashew nuts, ground roughly (optional)

Directions:
- Put the rice into a saucepan. Rinse the rice twice and discard the water.
- Add 250ml water and the pandan leaves, salam leaves, ginger, galangal and lemon grass and cook uncovered over a medium heat until the water has evaporated.
- If you have a rice steamer, transfer the rice into a steamer and steam over a medium heat for around 20 minutes. If not, turn down the heat into a low heat and cover the pan for 20 minutes. When it is cooked, transfer the rice into a large plate, set aside to cool.
- In the meantime prepare the coconut dressing. Heat a frying pan, add the oil, shallots and chillies and sauté for around 3-4 minutes. Add cumin, coriander and shrimp paste and cook for one minute. Add sliced lemon grass and the desiccated coconut, mix well and cook for around 5 minutes. Add the palm sugar and season with salt. Check the final seasoning, adding more salt if necessary.
- Remove the shells of the boiled eggs and halve each egg.
- To serve: mix the room temperature rice with the coconut dressing, add the sliced tomatoes, cucumber, half of the basil leaves and half of the fried shallots. Mix well and divide into four or six salad plates, add 2 sliced eggs and sprinkle with more basil leaves and fried shallots on top and serve immediately.

Fragrant rice cooked with coconut milk, ginger and lemon grass

NASI UDUK

This is similar to Nasi Lemak in Malaysian cuisine or Nasi Gurih from Aceh, Sumatra with a delicious rich flavour. It is cooked with coconut milk, lemon grass, lime leaves and salam (local bay leaves). Traditionally, it is served with many different small portions of side dishes, from fried chicken to peanut sambal for breakfast or lunch. I like to serve this with Jakarta style white chicken curry and a simple stirfried mixed vegetables.

Serves 4

- 250gr white rice
- 300ml coconut milk
- 2 sticks of lemon grass, crushed (the white part only and tied in a knot)
- 2 daun salam or bay leaves
- 2 lime leaves
- 1 tbsp whole coriander seeds roasted and ground finely
- 1 tsp salt

Peanut Sambal:
- 50gr raw skinless peanuts, roasted
- 5 curly chillies, ground finely

- 2 large red chillies grind finely
- 2 cloves of garlic, peeled and grated finely
- ½ tsp of sugar
- 1 tsp rice vinegar
- 2 tbsp coconut oil or vegetable oil
- 100ml water
- Salt to season

Side Dishes:
- Aromatic white chicken curry (see page 144)
- Fried shallots (see page 38)
- Prawn crackers (optional)
- Your favourite stir-fried vegetables

Directions:
- Rinse the rice and put it into a medium pan. Add the coconut cream and the rest of the rice ingredients. Cook until the liquid has evaporated and transfer the rice into a rice steamer. If you don't have a steamer, cook the rice for another 5 minutes in a low heat with the lid on. Turn the heat off. Keep the lid on and put aside for another 10-15 minutes until thoroughly cooked.
- To make the sambal: Heat a frying pan, add the garlic and chillies together and sauté for around 2-3 minutes. Add the rest of the ingredients and reduce the liquid until nearly dry. Season with salt. Check the seasoning and set aside to cool. Add the peanuts, mix well and set aside.
- To serve, make sure the rice, chicken and stir-fried vegetables are hot. Put the rice in the middle of each plate. Add a whole leg of white chicken curry and stir fried vegetables. Serve the peanut sambal on the side.

Meat, Poultry and Fish

Beef stew Betawi style

SEMUR DAGING

Enjoy the tender and succellent pieces of meat and delicious whole caramelized shallots in this dish of many different spices. I use plenty of shallots to create a pleasant texture for the sauce. The cooking process is long but worth the wait. Serve with steamed rice or pasta. Chopped tomatoes give the dish its vibrant colour and add well to the flavour combination.

Serves 4-6

Ingredients:
- 1kg stewing beef, cut into chunky pieces
- 300gr whole peeled shallots
- 20gr garlic, peeled
- 6 candlenuts
- 1 tsp freshly ground black pepper
- 1 tbsp ground coriander
- 1 tbsp ground cumin
- 1 tsp each ground nutmeg and cloves
- 10cm fresh ginger, peeled and ground
- 10cm fresh galangal, peeled and chopped roughly

Extra Ingredients:
- 2 sticks of cinnamon
- 6 cardamom
- 2 sticks of lemon grass (use the white part only, crushed roughly)
- 2 mace
- 4 lime leaves
- 5 tbsp of sweet soya sauce
- 500ml water
- 1 tbsp fried shallots (optional)

Directions:
- Slice half of the shallots and garlic. Grind finely together with candlenuts using a pestle and mortar. Set aside and keep half of the shallots whole.
- Rub the black pepper, ground coriander, cumin, nutmeg and cloves into the beef. Season the beef with salt. Mix in the ground shallots, nutmeg and candlenuts. Marinate for an hour in the refrigerator.
- Remove the marinated beef from the refrigerator 30 minutes before cooking.
- Heat a frying pan and add coconut oil or vegetable oil. Place the beef in the frying pan. You need to brown the meat in two or three batches depending on the amount of beef being cooked and the size of your frying pan.
- Heat a medium sized pan. Add 2 tbsp of coconut oil or vegetable oil and sauté the shallots, garlic and candlenut paste for around 3-4 minutes. Add the beef and mix well, then add 500ml water or home made beef stock.
- Cook over a low heat for around 2 hours and add the whole shallots to caramelize
- Taste the seasoning once more. Add more salt and black pepper if necessary.
- Serve with steamed rice or pasta with small cubes of tomato and sprinkle with deep-fried shallots.

Roasted chicken, Jakarta style

AYAM PANGGANG JAKARTA

This recipe is based on Jakarta fried chicken with herbs and spices. Although cooked with many different spices the taste of this dish is not spicy at all. It is ideally complemented by a mixed salad with dressing or simply served with steamed rice and your favourite stir-fried vegetables. I flatten the chicken first to ensure the cooking time is shortened. You don't need any gravy or 'sambal' at all. Enjoy the delicate mixture of roots, spices, lime, coriander and lemon grass.

Serves 4

Ingredients:
- 1 whole chicken, weighing around 1.3kg
- 2 tbsp lime juice
- 1 tsp freshly ground black pepper
- 1 tsp salt

For the Paste:
- 75gr shallots, peeled
- 4 cloves of garlic, peeled
- 5cm each of fresh ginger, turmeric, peeled, grated or sliced thinly; fresh chopped galangal or 1 tsp each of ginger, turmeric and galangal powder
- 2 candlenuts
- 1 tsp freshly ground black pepper
- 1 tbsp whole coriander seeds, roasted and ground
- 2 sticks of lemon grass, use the white part only, sliced thinly
- 1 tsp of salt
- 2 tbsp coconut oil or vegetable oil
- 1 tbsp lime juice

Directions:
- Preheat oven to 180°C.
- To make the paste: simply grind all the ingredients with a pestle and mortar or use a small food processor for a coarse mix
- Transfer the mixture into a medium bowl, season with salt. Add two tbsp of cooking oil and one tbsp lime juice.
- Cut along the backbone of the chicken with kitchen scissors or a sharp knife, and then press firmly down on the breastbone to flatten it. Dry the chicken using a kitchen towel
- Prick the flesh of the chicken with a sharp knife and season with salt, black pepper, lime; smear or rub the paste all over including the cavity of the chicken
- Place the chicken in a roasting tin or baking dish and cook for 50-60 minutes
- Remove the chicken from the oven and let it rest for around 10 minutes. Cut the chicken into four pieces and serve immediately.

White snapper fillet with black nut sauce served with pasta

FILLET IKAN KAKAP PUTIH PUCUNG

Traditionally, this fish dish uses freshwater fish called ikan gabus with plenty of soupy liquid. But instead I choose not to add big quantities of water in order to achieve a thicker sauce to serve with this snapper fillet and pasta. An alternative is to replace the capellini with rice to make black risotto without black ink squid, which is perfect for those who have a seafood allergy. You may experiment to replace the kluwak or black nut with a mixture of brown and black olives, It is important to blend or grind the olives into a fine paste. This is an easy dish to make, and sure to please a big crowd.

Serves 4-6

Ingredients:
- 4-6 white snapper fillets at around 120gr
- Juice of two limes; 2 tbsp of coconut oil or vegetable oil
- Salt and black pepper to taste
- 300-400g capellini
- 2 l water
- 2 tbsp sea salt (or regular salt)

For the Paste:
- 100g of shallots, peeled
- 4 cloves of peeled garlic
- 3 candlenuts
- 5 cm of fresh peeled turmeric
- 5 curly red chillies (add more if you like more spice) chopped roughly
- 1 tbsp of ground coriander
- 5 black nuts or keluak, crack the shell and remove the soft paste inside
- Juice of 1 lime
- 2 tbsp of coconut oil or any vegetable oil

Other Ingredients:
- 2 crushed lemon grass stalks, use the white part only
- 4 lime leaves; 2 bay leaves or daun salam
- 2 tomatoes deseeded and choped into small cubes
- 500ml water
- 1 tsp of sugar (optional)
- Salt and black pepper to taste

Directions:
- First, prepare the paste. Simply put all the ingredients into a small food processor and blend for a few minutes until you have a fine paste. Alternatively you can use a pestle and mortar to grind all the ingredients finely.
- Heat a frying pan and add two tbsp of oil. Add the paste and sauté for around 4-5 minutes or until fragrant.
- Add water, lemon grass and all the other ingredients (except the chopped tomatoes) and simmer for around 25-30 minutes or until you have a thick sauce. Season with salt.
- In the meantime prepare the fish and capellini.
- Bring water to boil in a medium pan and add 1 tbsp of olive oil. It takes only two minutes to cook the capellini so prepare the fish first.
- Season the fish with salt and lime juice. In the meantime, reheat the sauce.
- Heat a non-stick frying pan, add a tbsp of oil and cook the fish for around 3-5 minutes depending on the thickness of the fish. Season with black pepper and check the final taste.
- Cook the capellini for 2 minutes, strain.
- Divide the pasta into 4 or 6 individual serving dishes. Place the fish on top. Garnish with chopped tomatoes and add enough sauce to each dish and serve immediately.

Fish fillet with turmeric and chilli sauce

IKAN KAKAP PUTIH PESMOL

Traditionally made with whole freshwater milkfish (bandeng) but I use white snapper fillet or you can any type of white whole or fish fillet. The fish is deep fried first and the sauce made separately and added just before serving. I cook the fish with skin on and pan-fried on a high heat to crate a nice texture on the outside. Add to the sauce and cook for a few minutes on a low heat before serving. The fish will be very tender and the sauce will have a rich flavour from candlenuts. You may replace the candlenuts with macadamia or Brazilian nuts if preferred. I just love the vivid colour of this dish.

Serves 4

- 120gr x 4 white fish fillets
- 1-2 tbsp of lime juice
- Salt to season
- 2 red tomatoes, chopped into cubes
- 2 spring onions, sliced diagonally
- 2 large chillies, cut into 5 pieces
- 2-3 tbsp coconut oil or vegetable oil
- 200ml water or home made fish stock (see vegetable stock page 38)

For the Paste:

- 75gr shallots, peeled
- 4 cloves of garlic, peeled
- 100gr candlenuts
- 7gr both fresh ginger and galangal, peeled and chopped roughly
- 4gr aromatic ginger (kencur), peeled and chopped roughly
- 1-tbsp coriander seeds, roasted
- 3 red birds eye chillies

Directions:

- Grind the coriander seeds finely with pestle and mortar. You may grind the rest of the ingredients with pestle and mortar or simply put them into a chopper or blender and process it into a fine paste. Set aside.
- Heat a deep-frying pan and add the paste and cook for around 6-8 minutes, stirring occasionally. Add water or fish stock and cook in medium heat until the sauce has a creamy consistency. Season with salt.
- In the meantime, season the fish with salt and lime juice.
- Heat a frying pan and add 2 or 3 tbsp of coconut oil or vegetable oil and place the fish skin down in the hot oil. Cook for
  3 minutes on the skin side and 2 minutes on the other side.
- While the fish is cooking, add tomatoes, spring onions and large chillies and cook for 1-2 minutes.
- Remove from the pan and transfer the fish into the sauce mixture and cook for another 1-2 minutes on low heat. Check to make sure the fish is cooked thoroughly but still soft and moist.
- Transfer the fish onto individual plates or a large serving plate and serve with simple stir-fried vegetables and steamed rice or simply with pasta.

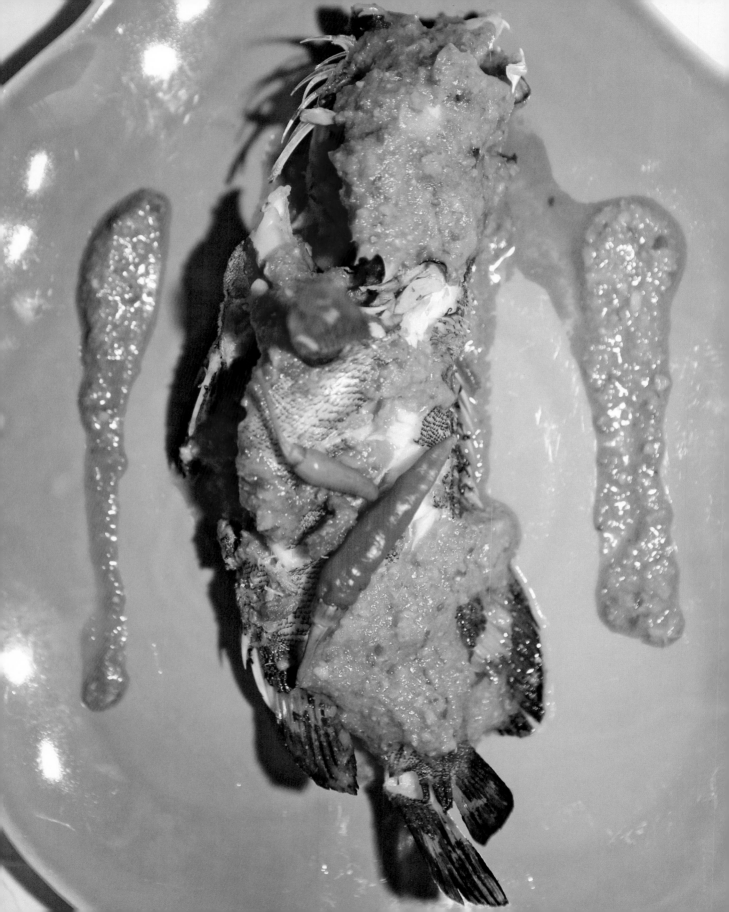

Whole steamed coral trout with chillies and ginger sauce

KERAPU PECAK KUKUS

Traditionally, freshwater fish such as lele (cat fish), gabus or gurame is used for this dish but such varieties are not always readily available, so alternatives such as trout, barramundi or any white fish will work just as well. The traditional recipe involves deep-frying the fish but I have chosen to steam the fish for this recipe, adding the chilli and ginger sauce.

Serves 4

Ingredients:
- 400gr x 4 whole coral trout fish or rainbow trout for individual serving or 150gr x 4 cod or barramundi fillets (or any white fish)
- Juice of 2 limes
- Salt to season
- 2 cloves of garlic, peeled and grated
- 50gr shallots, peeled and sliced finely
- 5gr ginger, peeled and grated

For the Sauce:
- 5 cloves of garlic, peeled
- 75gr of shallots, peeled
- 5gr both ginger and galangal, peeled and chopped roughly
- 4 birds eye chilies (add more for a spicier taste)
- 3 tbsp coconut oil or vegetable oil
- Juice of 1 lime
- ½ tsp sugar
- ½ tsp white pepper
- 1 tablespoon of lime juice
- 500ml water
- 50ml cooking oil
- Salt to season

Directions:
- Score each fish piece with a knife and season with salt, lime and rub with garlic, ginger and shallots. Set aside to marinade while preparing the sauce.
- In the meantime, heat a frying pan and add whole shallots, garlic, chillies, ginger and galangal and cook for around 10 minutes over a medium heat, stirring occasionally. You are looking to caramelize the shallots to give this dish a sweet taste.
- Turn the heat off. Transfer the ingredients into a blender, add water and blend. Transfer the mixture back to the same frying pan.
- Heat a large round steamer, and over a low-medium heat cook the fish for 10-12 minutes thoroughly but ensuring it remains moist and tender
- Reheat the sauce and season with salt, white pepper and limejuice, reduce to half and check the final seasoning.
- When the fish is cooked, place each of the fish on an individual dish, and pour on the sauce. Serve with steamed rice and your favourite stir-fried vegetables.

Iconic Regional Dishes Featured Among Jakarta's Food Vendors

Seafood

Tekwan with red mackerel and prawns

TEKWAN DARI PALEMBANG

Medium sized fresh mackerel and prawns take only one and a half to two minutes to cook. The Jicama or Mexican turnip, known locally as bengkuang is a very low calorie root vegetable said to be a fine source of dietary fibre and anti-oxidants and to preserve its crunchy texture I serve it raw in this dish. If you use dried ear mushrooms it is important to soak them first in hot water for 3-4 minutes. In the broth I feature dried Polianthes tuberosa a very popular long lasting cut flower that smells delicious, originally from Mexico and was grown by the Aztecs. In the south of France vast areas of tuberosa supply the perfume industry.

Serves 6

Ingredients:
- 200 gr mackerel or tenggiri fillet fish, cut into 2 cm cubes
- 18 medium prawns. Clean the heads and keep the shells

For the Fish Balls:
- 300 gr mackerel or tenggiri fillet
- 2 egg whites
- 2 tbsp tapioca or sago flour
- 1 clove of garlic, peeled and ground or grated finely
- 1 small spring onion, sliced finely

- 1/2 tsp freshly ground white pepper season with salt
- 2 litres of water

For the Broth:
- 4 cloves of garlic, peeled and ground finely
- 50 gr shallots, peeled and ground finely
- 14 strings of dried polianthes and tuberosa (optional), tying each string into a knot
- 50 gr fresh or 20 gr dried ear mushroom
- small bunch of flat parsley
- 1 bengkuang or Jicama or Mexican turnip, peeled and cut into long thin strips

- ½ tsp of sugar
- 4 tbsp lime juice season with salt and white pepper

Other Ingredients:
- 100 gr transparent or glass noodles, soaked in hot water for 3-4 minutes and refreshed with cold water. Strain and set aside
- 75 gr shallots, peeled, finely sliced, seasoned with salt and deep fried
- Small bunch of flat parsley, chopped finely
- Green or red chillies, sliced
- Lime juice

Directions:
- To make the prawn stock heat one tbsp of coconut oil or vegetable oil in a large pan over medium heat. Add the shrimp shells and heads, toss well. Cook for 2-3 minutes and add 2 litres of water. Bring to a boil, simmer for 30 minutes.
- To make the fish balls, put the fish fillet in a food processor and process until the mixture turns to fine paste. Add the rest of the ingredients and process until combined well. In the meantime, boil 2 litres of water in a large pan.
- Transfer the fish mixture into a medium bowl. Using two small spoons, make small balls until all the mixture is finished. Put the fish balls into the boiled water and cook until they float to the top. Set aside.
- To make the broth, heat one tbsp of oil and add the garlic and shallot paste. Cook for 30 seconds. Add the 1.5 litres of hot prawn stock, the dried polianthes tuberosa and flat parsley. Cook on low heat for 15 minutes. Season with salt and pepper.
- Add the ear mushroom. Cook for an extra 2-3 minutes.
- Add the prawns and sliced fish fillet and cook for 1-2 minutes. Add lime juice.
- To serve, divide the noodles into six individual serving bowls, add the fish balls and sliced fish fillet. Add the jicama, prawns and pour the broth on top. Sprinkle with chopped flat parsley, chopped chillies if you wish and fried shallots. Serve hot.

Angel hair with Manadonese mixed seafood in woku blanga sauce

BARAMUNDI WOKU BLANGA

Why not be different and serve this Indonesian dish with pasta and not with a bowl of rice. This is a delightful dish with multilayers of flavours from ginger, chillies, lemon grass, basil, tomatoes and seafood.

Serves 4

- 250g white snapper or any white fish fillet, sliced into chunky bite sized pieces
- 250gr medium prawns, shells removed
- 150gr squid, cut into ½ cm thickness rings
- 2 tbsp lime juice
- 1 tsp salt

For the Paste:
- 5 birds eye chillies, roughly chopped (use more chillies for a more spicy taste)
- 5gr fresh turmeric, roughly chopped (replace with 1 tsp turmeric powder)

- 10gr fresh ginger, roughly chopped (replace with 1 tbsp ginger powder)
- 5gr fresh galangal, roughly chopped (replace with 1 tsp galangal powder)
- 100gr shallots, roughly chopped
- 3 garlic cloves
- 2 candlenuts or 30gr macadamia nuts (optional)

Other Ingredients:
- 2 lemongrass stalks, crushed
- 2 spring onions, roughly chopped
- 1 *pandan* leaf and turmeric leaves (optional)

- 1kg red tomatoes, chopped finely
- 2 lime leaves
- A handful of kemangi, Indonesian basil but may be replaced with Italian basil, roughly chopped
- Salt to taste
- 3 tbsp olive oil or any coconut oil or vegetable oil
- 1 tbsp lime juice
- Salt and black pepper to taste

For the Pasta:
- 200-250gr-angel hair pasta
- Plenty of salted boiling water

Directions:
- Put the chillies, ginger, shallots, garlic, galangal, candlenuts and turmeric into a food processor and process until the mixture becomes a fine paste.
- Heat the olive oil in a large thick-bottomed pan. When hot, add the paste and cook for 5-7 minutes or until fragrant.
- Add the lemon grass, spring onions, tomatoes, pandan leaf and half of the basil to the paste.
- Cook for 10 minutes on low-medium heat. Stir from time to time. Season with salt.
- While the tomato sauce is cooking, season the fish and prawns (not the squid) with salt and lime juice as a quick marinade for about 1-2 minutes.
- Add the fish and prawns, cook and simmer for 2-3 minutes. Cover with a lid during the cooking process. Then add the squid and cook for 1-2 minutes. Add basil and lime juice.
- In the meantime, cook the pasta in generous amounts of boiling salted water until al dente for a maximum of 2 minutes.
- Check the final seasoning. Add a touch of salt and lime juice if necessary. Discard the lemon grass stalks and lime leaves.
- Drain the pasta, keeping a little of the pasta water. Add the pasta and retained pasta water to the sauce in the pan and toss gently together.
- Divide the pasta onto 4 serving plates and garnish with basil and serve hot immediately.

Acehnese barramundi fillet curry with a twist

GULAI BARRAMUNDI DENGAN ASAM SUNTI DARI ACEH

This refreshing curry offers a wonderful infusion of fennel, coriander seeds curry and pandan leaves, with the tangy taste of belimbing wuluh or sour finger carambola (a member of the star fruit family) and lime juice. Belimbing wuluh fruit can be eaten raw, dipped in rock salt but, as in this dish, are frequently curried. This recipe calls for dried belimbing wuluh, known locally as asam sunti, but if not available you can simply use lime or lemon for the required acidity. The dish is notable for its creamy texture and vibrant yellow and orange hues. And you can substitute most white fish if barramundi is hard to find.

Serves 4

Ingredients:
- 4 pieces of 150gr barramundi fillet
- Salt to season
- Juice of 1 lime
- 2 tbsp coconut oil or vegetable oil
- 250ml or 1 tin coconut milk
- 100ml water

For the Paste:
- 3 cloves of garlic, peeled
- 75gr shallots, peeled and chopped roughly
- 7gr fresh turmeric and ginger, peeled and chopped roughly
- 8 curly red chillies, chopped roughly

Other Ingredients:
- 1 tbsp each of roasted coriander and fennel seeds, finely ground
- 1 tsp freshly ground black pepper
- 2 red tomatoes, chopped into cubes
- 4 belimbing wuluh (sour finger carambola) chopped roughly
- the juice of 2 limes
- 1 pandan leaf, chopped roughly
- A small bunch of curry leaves
- 2 tbsp coconut oil or vegetable oil

Directions:
- Grind the ingredients for the paste finely. Set aside
- Heat a frying pan. Add the coconut oil or vegetable oil and paste and fry for 2-3 minutes. Stir continuously.
- Add the ground coriander and fennel seeds and cook for 30 seconds
- Add the chopped tomatoes, sliced belimbing wuluh, pandan leaves and curry leaves. Mix well and sauté for 30 seconds. Then add the water and season with salt. Bring to a boil and simmer on low heat for 15 minutes to allow the flavours to infuse.
- Add the coconut milk, bring to the boil, simmer and season with salt.
- Season the fish fillets with salt and lime juice. Add the fillets to the mixture and cook on each side for 3-4 minutes, depending on the thickness. Check the final seasoning.
- Transfer the fish and the sauce to one large serving plate or smaller dishes as individual servings. Add the sauce and serve immediately with steamed white or brown rice and some steamed vegetables.

Grilled Fish with lime and chillies

IKAN BAKAR DENGAN JERUK DAN CABE

Grilled or barbecued fish in a country with 17,000 islands promises lots of variety, region to region from sweet Javanese styles to spicy preferred in Manado. Variations include a rica-rica marinade, yellow turmeric paste a favourite among the Sundanese or with a touch of sweet soya sauce and chopped green chillies.

It is important to ensure the dish has a touch of acidity by marinating in tamarind or lime juice. The classic way is to use coconut husk or dried coconut shell to grill or barbecue fish which gives it a distinctive smoky flavour. The classic approach is to use the whole fish, but for this recipe I chose fillets of local barramundi. Most white fish can be substituted and I sometimes use salmon fillet for something different, served with simple mixed salad dressing for a nutritious light meal.

Serves 4

Ingredients:

- 4 fillets barramundi at 150gr each
- 50gr shallots, peeled and chopped roughly
- 3 cloves of garlic, peeled and chopped roughly
- 2 candlenuts
- 2 bird's eye chillies
- 1 tablespoons palm sugar or brown sugar
- 2 tablespoons lime juice
- 3 tablespoons extra virgin coconut oil or vegetable oil
- Salt to taste

The extra sauce:

- Sweet soya sauce and chopped chillies

Directions:

- Prepare a barbeque (traditional charcoal is preferred but a modern BBQ works well).
- Grind the cloves, shallots, candlenuts and chilies into a fine paste with a pestle and mortar.
- Add the palm sugar, 2 tablespoons lime juice and season with salt.
- Mix well and set aside.
- Season the fish with salt, black pepper and rub the paste over the fish and set aside to marinate for 30 minutes.
- To grill, simply put the fillet fishes over the charcoal turning every 30-45 seconds for around 8-10 minutes depending on the thickness of the fish.
- Baste with the paste once or twice
- Serve with steamed rice or simple salad and sambal kecap on the side if you wish.

Raw Tuna with calamansi, chilli and kemangi

GOHU IKAN

This is not usually found in the streets of Jakarta but instead in remote Maluku or North Sulawesi island. I have chosen to include this dish as it is simple, easy to make and is absolutely delicious. It is very important to use the freshest tuna.

Serves 4

Ingredients:
- 200 gr tuna fillet of sashimi quality

Dressing:
- 1 large papaya chili peppper and 2 birds eye red chilli, sliced
- 50 gr shallots, peeled and chopped
- A bunch of kemangi or local basil, chopped
- Juice of 3-4 calamansi or 2 limes
- Salt
- Kemangi leaves or basil and edible flowers for garnish (optional)

You also need 4 serving plates, chilled in the refrigerator for around one hour prior.

Directions:
- Put the sliced chili, chopped shallots and basil into a medium bowl. Add the calamansi juice and season with salt.
- Slice the tuna fillet with thin slices around 0.2cm thickness.
- Place 3 sliced tuna on each of the cold plates.
- Season the tuna with salt and drizzle and spread each of the tuna fillets with the dressing and garnish with micro basil and edible flowers just for fun. Serve immediately.

Fillet of white snapper arsik from North Sumatera

IKAN ARSIK DENGAN KAKAP PUTIH

Arsik is a classic dish from the Batak Community of North Sumatra traditionally using a whole carp but for this recipe I have substituted red snapper. You can substitute other fish as you wish, even prawns. There are several exotic ingredients needed: kecombrang (ginger flowers) and asam cekala/buah kecombrang (fruit of the ginger flower), bawang Batak/lokio (baby spring onions), and asam gelugur (preserved gelugur fruit that has been sliced and dried in the sun). Last but not least is andaliman, or Sumatran Sichuan pepper. The totally unique fragrance of the ginger flower makes this dish so special. Outside Indonesia finding both the ginger flower and the fruit of the ginger flower is a challenge.

Traditionally, small eggplants and long beans are added into the dish. To make it 100% vegetarian, use tempe or tofu and vegetables such as eggplants, long beans and/or young French beans. You can serve this recipe as a main dish with steamed rice or as a soup. You just add more water and adjust the seasoning but please note it is important to first allow almost all the liquid to evapourate in cooking to infuse the flavour of all the herbs and spices properly, before adding water to make soup.

Serves 4

Ingredients:
- 4 fillets of white snapper @ 150gr
- 2 tbsp lime juice
- Salt to season

Paste:
- 5 red birdseye chillies
- 3 red curly chillies
- 3 candlenuts
- 3 cloves of garlic
- 75gr shallots

- 7gr fresh ginger and turmeric (replace with 1 tsp dried ginger and turmeric)
- 7gr fresh galangal or you can replace with 4-5 slices of dried galangal (first soak in hot water)

Other Ingredients:
- 2 ginger flowers or kecombrang, sliced round and thinly
- 4 buah kecombrang/asam cekala, cut into halves (optional)

- 4 lime leaves
- 2 lemon grass stalks, crushed and tied in a knot
- 5 pieces asam gelugur
- Small bunch of bawang Batak/lokio or simply replace with small spring onion
- 2 tbsp dried andaliman, finely ground
- 1-2 tbsp lime juice
- salt to taste

Directions:
- Grind the ingredients for the paste. Put 500ml hot water in a pan or wok and add the paste. Cook at medium-high heat for 10-12 minutes until the liquid is reduced.
- Add sliced ginger flower and the rest of the ingredients except the fish and 500ml hot water. Season with salt. Cook for another 15 minutes to infuse all the ingredients.
- Season the fish with lime juice and salt. Add the fish into the mixture. Cover the pan or wok. Cook over low-medium heat for around 8-10 minutes but be careful not to overcook the fish, as this will produce a dry and chewy texture.
- To serve, place each of the fish fillets on a pasta dish or bowl, divide the vegetables and the sauce. Serve hot with a small portion of rice in the bowl or on the side.

Barbequed King Prawns with Borneo mango sambal

UDANG BAKAR DENGAN SAMBAL RAJA

This sambal is unusual in its ingredients, which include boiled eggs, cooked long beans and eggplant. I have used limes in this recipe while the original calls for the very popular citrus fruit 'lemon cui' or 'jeruk kesturi.' Otherwise known as calamansi it is a trusted ingredient in Manado, North Sulawesi, particularly popular in seafood but also meat dishes. It is also used ingredient in the dabu dabu sambal, one of the favourite condiments of this region.

Serves 4

Ingredients:
- 16 king prawns
- Juice of 2 limes
- ½ tsp of salt
- 2 tbsp of cooking oil

For the Sambal:
- 15 long red chillies
- 8 shallots
- 1 large tomato (chopped)

- 1 tbsp of sugar
- 1 tbsp spoon palm sugar syrup
- ½ to 1 tsp "shrimp paste". You can buy ready-to-use shrimp paste in any local supermarket or you can substitute 1-2 anchovies depending on personal taste
- 2 tbsp coconut oil or vegetable oil
- 1 small unripe mango (skinned and grated)

Directions:
- First prepare the sambal. Using a pestle and mortar grind the chillies and shallots until fine. Add the shrimp paste then the chopped tomato. Heat a frying pan. Add the oil then the paste. Cook for 5 minutes. Add the sugar, palm sugar syrup and salt. Cook for another 5 minutes on a low heat and set aside.
- Preparing the king prawns. Cut the prawns in half, including the head of the prawn then wash under running water. Cook on the barbecue or griddle pan for around 5-6 minutes. Serve with mango sambal and steamed rice.

Tagliatelle with Manado Tuna 'Rica-rica'

TAGLIATELLE DENGAN TUNA RICA-RICA

Rica-rica is one of the most spicy cooking styles favoured in Manado. It combines chillies shallots and ginger and I prefer to add tomatoes. Rica is a local term used to mean spicy or chilli, and is synonymous with the cuisine of this region. For this recipe I use tinned tuna for convenience and a great result. Also I don't mind to use olive oil on this recipe.

Serves 4

Ingredients:
- 250 gr dried tagliatelle
- 1 tin of tuna (discard the water)

For the Sauce:
- 20 shallots, peeled and sliced thinly
- 5-7 red curly chillies, ground
- 10 centimeters fresh ginger, peeled and grated
- 2 cloves of garlic
- a small bunch of kemangi (local basil)
- 20 cherry tomatoes, cut into halves
- 4 tbsp olive oil (2 tbsp for sautéing and 2 for drizzling)
- juice of 1-2 limes
- 3-4 tbsp water
- Salt to taste.

Directions:
- Bring 1.5 litres water to the boil. Add 1 tbsp salt. Add pasta to boiling water and cook according to directions on the package.
- While the water is coming to a boil, heat 2 tbsp olive oil in a frying pan, then add shallots and garlic. Sauté for around 2-3 minutes or until soft, then add ground chillies and ginger and cook for another 3-4 minutes, stirring from time to time.
- Season the tuna with salt and lime juice. Cook for around 4-5 minutes, then add half of the chopped cherry tomatoes and cook for another 2 minutes.
- Drain the pasta, transfer into the pan and add the rest of the tomatoes and torn basil. Season with salt and toss the mixture together. If it is too dry, add several tbsp of water and 1-2 tbsp of oil to give a nice glossy finish. Mix well.
- Divide the pasta between 4 serving plates. Garnish with basil leaves and serve immediately.

Otak-otak with cucumber and carrots

OTAK-OTAK

I like to serve the otak-otak in a modern way as part of a salad dish. To simplify the otak otak. I don't cook it in a banana leaf, as is the norm. Instead, I put the mixture into small ramekins to make individual fish cakes and cook them in the oven.

Serves 6

Ingredients for the Fish:
- 250 gr white snapper fillets, red snapper or any white fish fillet
- 2 tbsp coconut cream
- Salt and black pepper to season

Ingredients for the Paste:
- 2 lemon grass stalks chopped finely (discard the outer green layer, use white parts only)
- 5 cm turmeric
- 10 shallots, peeled
- 3 candlenuts
- 5 large dried red chillies soaked in hot water until soft
- ½ tsp roasted shrimp paste (optional)
- 1 tbsp coriander seeds, roasted and ground
- ½ tsp sugar
- 2 tbsp coconut oil or vegetable oil

Ingredients for the Salad:
- 2 medium cucumbers, peeled and sliced thinly
- 3 medium carrots, peeled and grated
- A small bunch of kemangi or local basil, using leaves only

Ingredients for the Peanut Sauce:
- 100 gr of raw peanuts, roasted on a dry frying pan in low heat
- 2 or 3 large red dried chillies, soaked in hot water
- ½ clove of garlic
- 100 millilitres water
- 2 to 3 tbsp white wine vinegar or apple cider vinegar
- ¼ tsp sugar
- Salt to taste

Directions:
- To make the fish cakes: grind all the paste ingredients finely. Set aside.
- Chop the fish into small cubes and put in the food processor and process until the mixture has become fine in texture.
- Heat a frying pan and add 2 tbsp of coconut oil or vegetable oil. Add the paste and cook for 4-5 minutes or until fragrant. Transfer the mixture to a plate to cool.
- Pre-heat the oven to 180°C.
- Add the paste mixture into the food processor. Add an egg and the coconut cream. Season with salt and black pepper and process the mixture finely
- Smear the inside of the ramekins with coconut oil or vegetable oil. Divide the mixture into six portions and put into 7cm ramekins. Then place the ramekins on a baking tray and cook in the oven for 20-25 minutes.
- While the otak-otak is in the oven, prepare the sauce by grinding the peanuts and mixing well with the rest of the ingredients. The texture of the sauce should be creamy, not too thick or too runny. Season with salt if necessary.

To serve:
- Place the grated carrots in the middle of six serving plates.
- Place the sliced cucumber around the carrots.
- Add the peanut sauce and some basil leaves.
- Lastly, place the fish cake on the top. Serve immediately.

Bandung dumplings with spicy peanut sauce

SIOMAY BANDUNG

A very popular dish, influenced by Chinese dumplings but offers totally different flavours with the addition of tofu, boiled potatoes and some vegetables served with a tangy spicy peanut sauce.

Serves 8

Ingredients:

For the Seafood Dumpling:
- 200gr fillet of mackerel, chopped roughly
- 200gr prawns (head and shell discarded and set aside), chopped roughly
- 50gr carrots, grated finely
- 5 cloves of garlic, peeled
- 50gr shallots, peeled
- 1 tbsp chopped chives
- 12 Wonton skins
- Salt and freshly ground white pepper

For the Peanut Sauce:
- 200gr roasted peanuts
- 25gr red birds eye chillies, boiled and chopped roughly
- 50ml vinegar
- 2 cloves garlic, finely ground
- 1 tbsp sugar
- 200ml water

Extra Ingredients:
- 100gr tofu, steamed or boiled and cut into 8 pieces
- 4 pieces of cabbage leaves, steamed rolled (like spring rolls) and sliced
- 1 large bitter gourd
- 4 soft-boiled eggs, cut into halves (optional)

Condiments:
- Sweet soya sauce
- Tomato sauce (optional)
- Slice of lime or kaffir lime

Directions:
- Put all the ingredients for the seafood dumpling (except chives and carrots) into a blender or a food processor. Blend well and season with salt and white pepper. If you don't have a food processor or blender, simply mince the fish and prawns finely and mix with finely chopped shalots, garlic and the rest of the ingredients.
- Put aside ¼ of the mixture for filling the bitter gourd.
- Add the grated carrots and chopped chives and mix well in a large bowl.
- Return the seafood mixture into the bowl, continue this slapping until the mixture becomes firmer and stickier to give a more fluffy texture when steamed.
- Mold the dumpling in small balls and steam for around 10 minutes.
- For the bitter gourd, steam or blanch for 1 minute or until soft then remove, cool and slice in approximately 1.5cm thickness.
- To make the sauce, simply put all the ingredients into a blender, blend well and check the seasoning. Season with salt. You need to a sweet, spicy and sour creamy texture for peanut sauce.
- To serve: place one or two pieces of dumpling, tofu, steamed cabbage and sliced bitter gourd pieces. Drizzle the sauce around the dumplings and vegetables. Add a touch of sweet soya sauce and tomato sauce if needed. Serve hot.

Rice, Noodles, Laksa and Soto

Fried Rice

To Indonesians, Nasi Goreng or fried rice is as loved as pasta or pizza by Italians or fish and chips among the British. And it is the most obvious proof of Chinese influences on Indonesian cuisine. Nasi goreng can be found everywhere – from street vendors to coffee shops and five star hotel restaurants in Jakarta. Indonesia is the third largest rice producer in the world and its citizens show a voracious appetite, consuming almost 130 kilogrammes per person every year – no wonder Nasi Goreng has become a national dish!

The classic nasi goreng offers a range of complex flavours from a base of chillies, shallots and garlic, plus ingredients such as shrimp paste (terasi), sweet soya sauce, salted fish, seafood, chicken, eggs, stinky beans (known as pete) and even goat's meat. Popular toppings include fried eggs sunny side up, various types of sate or fried chicken, depending on the regional origin or speciality of the street vendor.

A good nasi goreng should be light, moist and fluffy with the rice grains separate. It should look an attractive from the different colours of ingredients. I prefer to have plenty of protein versus rice providing a variety of taste without making my guests feel too full.

There are certain rules to follow, the main one uses day-old leftover rice from the previous night – which makes the dish a popular option for breakfast. As a child in Manado, North Sulawesi I recall my grandmother's explanation that cooking the rice with extra ingredients brings out and enhances the flavours of the dish. Another rule is to take the rice at room temperature and mix it with other ingredients once they are almost cooked, then allow the cooking process to continue after the rice is added. And for truly traditional eating, serve this dish with 'kerupuk' or crackers of rice or shrimp, which add texture and flavour to the whole experience.

Clockwise from top left: Village Fried Rice; Goat Fried Rice; Padang Pesto Fried Rice with Shrimps; and Seafood Fried Rice.

Village fried rice

NASI GORENG KAMPUNG

This is the basic and the most affordable fried rice with chillies, shallots, garlic, shrimp paste and eggs. It is a good idea to add plenty of vegetables to give a good balance and I have added carrots and pakcoy.

Serves 4

- 800gr leftover rice
- 4 eggs, lightly beaten
- 75gr shallots, peeled and sliced thinly
- 4 cloves of garlic, peeled and chopped roughly
- 4 birds-eye chillies, chopped roughly
- 1 tsp roasted shrimp paste or replace with 2 tbsp fish sauce

- 100gr carrots, peeled and grated
- 100gr pakchoy, sliced thinly lengthways
- 4 tbsp sweet soya sauce
- 4 coconut oil or vegetable oil
- Salt and white pepper to taste
- Pickled carrots and cucumber (see page 37)
- Rice crackers or shrimp crackers (optional)

Directions:
- Finely grind the chillies, garlic and roasted shrimp paste with pestle and mortar and set aside.
- Crack the eggs into a medium bowl and season with salt and freshly ground white pepper. Heat a wok or frying pan and add 2 tbsp of oil and scramble the eggs for 2-3 minutes (but not overcooked). Transfer into a bowl and set aside.
- Using the same wok or frying pan, add extra 2 tbsp of oil and sauté the paste for about 4-5 minutes. Add the rice and mix well for around 6-8 minutes, stirring from time to time. Season with salt.
- Make sure the rice grains do not stick together but are separated. Use a fork to separate lumpy rice.
- Add the vegetables and cook for around 1-2 minutes. Add a tbsp of water if the mixture is too dry.
- Add the eggs and mix well.
- Check the final seasoning. Add a touch of salt if necessary.
- To serve: Divide the fried rice into 4 serving plates garnished with grated carrots and sliced cabbage. Pickled cucumber and carrots and crackers on the side. Serve immediately.

Chicken fried rice with chillies and vegetables

NASI GORENG AYAM

It is very easy to cook this as long as you have prepared all the ingredients. If you do not have leftover rice, you may use fresh cooked rice but let the rice completely cool down to room temperature before cooking. The ginger flower provides a delicious flavour and fragrance. No soya sauce is required for this dish.

Serves 4

- 600gr cooked rice
- 600gr chicken breast, cut into strips around 3cm long with ½cm width
- 2 tbsp lime juice
- 120gr carrots, cut into small cubes
- 120gr French bean, cut into 1cm lengths
- Salt and ground black pepper to season

For the Paste:
- 4 cloves of garlic, peeled, crushed and chopped finely
- 100gr of shallots, peeled and sliced finely or replaced with 1 large onion, chopped

- 3 red bird eye chillies and 3 curly chillies, ground finely (add more for a spicier taste or reduce for mildness)
- 7gr fresh ginger, peeled and grated finely
- 1 tsp roasted shrimp paste or replace with 2 tbsp fish sauce, ground finely with chillies
- 2 ginger flowers. Remove the tough layers of the ginger flower buds and chop finely
- 3 tbsp of coconut oil or vegetable oil
- 4 tbsp water if needed

Directions:
- Season the chicken with salt and lime juice.
- Heat a frying pan. Add the oil, shallots and garlic and sauté for 2-3 minutes. Add the chillies, shrimp paste and ginger and sauté for around 2-3 minutes.
- Add the chicken and cook for around 5-6 minutes, stirring all the time.
- Add the rice and mix well. Season with salt. It will take around 3-4 minutes. Make sure the rice grains do not stick together but are separated. Use a fork and press to separate lumpy rice.
- Add the vegetables and cook for around 1-2 minutes. Add a tbsp of water if the mixture is too dry.
- Check the final seasoning. Add a touch of salt if necessary.
- To serve: Divide the fried rice into 4 serving plates. Garnish with grated carrots, thinly sliced chillies and ginger flower and serve immediately.

Padang pesto fried rice with shrimps

NASI GORENG SAMBAL IJO DAN UDANG

This dish offers the inviting flavour combination of green chillies with basil and the saltiness of the fish. You can substitute anchovies if salted fish is not available.

- 600gr cooked rice
- 300gr medium shrimps, shell discharged
- 2 tbsp lime juice
- A small bunch of kemangi, basil leaves
- 50gr good quality salted fish
- Salt and black pepper to season

For the *Bumbu*:
- 4 cloves of garlic, peeled, crushed and chopped finely

- 100gr of shallots, peeled and sliced finely or replaced with 1 large onion, chopped
- 3 green birds eye chillies and 3 curly chillies, ground finely (add more for spicier taste or reduce for mildness)
- 1 tsp roasted shrimp paste or replace with 2 tbsp fish sauce, ground finely with chillies
- 3 tbsp of coconut oil or vegetable oil
- 4 tbsp water if needed

Directions:
- Season the shrimps with salt and lime juice.
- Heat a frying pan. Add the oil, shallots and garlic and sauté for 2-3 minutes. Add the chillies, shrimp paste, sauté for around 2-3 minutes.
- Add the shrimps and cook for around 2-3 minutes, stirring all the time.
- Add the rice, salted fish and mix well. Season with salt. It will take around 3-4 minutes. Make sure the rice grains do not stick together but are separated. Use a fork to separate lumpy rice.
- Add the basil leaves and cook further for around 1-2 minutes. Add a tbsp of water if the mixture is too dry.
- Check the final seasoning. Add a touch of salt if necessary.
- To serve: Divide the fried rice into 4 serving plates. Garnish with basil leaves, and serve immediately.

Seafood fried rice

NASI GORENG SEAFOOD

This has more oriental flavours with ginger, soya sauce and sesame oil.

Serves 4-6

Ingredients:
- 600gr left over rice or cold freshly cooked rice
- 150gr medium prawns, shells removed
- 150gr skinless white snapper fillet or any other white fish, cut into 1cm pieces
- 2 tbsp each of sweet soya sauce and salted soya sauce
- 2-3 tbsp sesame oil
- 1 tsp freshly ground white pepper
- 50gr shallots, sliced thinly
- 1 medium spring onion, sliced thinly
- 4 cloves of garlic, peeled and chopped finely
- 5gr fresh ginger, peeled and grated
- 2-3 tbsp coconut oil or vegetable oil
- salt and white pepper to season
- 4 eggs (fried sunny side up)
- For garnish: fresh grated carrots

Directions:
- Season the seafood separately in each bowl with salt and white pepper. Heat a wok or deep frying pan and add 2-3 tbsp of oil. Cook the prawns for 2 minutes, stirring all the time. Transfer into a bowl. Add the fish and cook for 1 minute each side and transfer onto a plate. Set aside.
- In the same wok or deep-frying pan, add one tbsp extra oil. Add the shallots and garlic, ginger and sauté for 2-3 minutes. Add half of the chopped spring onions and the rice. Mix well. If the mixture is too dry, add 1-2 tbsp water.
- Add the soya sauces and season with salt and white pepper.
- Add all the seafood and mix well.
- Lastly, add the sesame oil and mix well. Transfer the rice into four or six individual plates or large serving plate for family style meal. Sprinkle with chopped spring onions and add each egg on top of the rice. Serve immediately.

Fried rice with goat meat spices and sweet soya sauce

NASI GORENG KAMBING

There is a famous vendor in Jalan Kebon Sirih, central Jakarta who sells goat fried rice, nasi goreng kambing Kebon Sirih. This is truly a fusion of flavours of Middle Eastern and Indonesian food, with many layers of spices and sweet soya sauce. I prefer to use goat tenderloin. You may replace it with beef tenderloin, lamb, beef or chicken. You can also create a perfect vegetarian fried rice with roasted eggplants.

Serves 4-6

- 800gr left over rice or cold freshly cooked rice
- 500gr goat tenderloin, cut into 1cm pieces
- 50ml water
- 3 tbsp coconut oil or vegetable oil
- 100gr shallots or replaced with 1 large onion, sliced thinly
- 3 cloves of garlic
- 1 tsp each of cumin and coriander seeds, roasted and ground finely
- 2 cardamoms, roasted and ground finely

- 4 red birds eye chillies, sliced finely or replace with 1tsp spice chilli powder
- 1 tsp of clove powder
- 1 tsp of cinnamon powder
- 2 salam or bay leaves
- 3 tbsp of sweet soya sauce
- Salt and black pepper to taste
- Juice of 1 lime
- 2 tbsp crunchy fried shallots – (see page 38)
- A small bunch of mint leaves, and some extra for garnish

Directions:
- Season the goat meat pieces with salt and black pepper.
- Heat a wok or frying pan and add 2 tbsp cooking oil. Add the meat and leave it for 1-2 minutes unstirred. Turn the meat pieces over and cook for another minute unstirred to have a nice texture on the outside of the meat, and juicy and tender on the inside. Transfer onto a plate and set aside.
- Add one extra tbsp of coconut oil or vegetable oil. Add the garlic and sauté for one minute. Add sliced shallots or onion and sauté for around 3-4 minutes. Stir from time to time.
- Add the spices, clove and cinnamon powder, cumin, coriander, chillies and cardamom and sauté for 30 seconds. Add the rice and mix well.
- Add 2-3 tbsp of water and sweet soya sauce. Mix well. Season with salt and black pepper. Make sure the rice grains do not stick together but are separated. Use a fork to separate lumpy rice.
- Add the meat, including the juices and cook for another 3-4 minutes.
- Add lime juice and fresh mint leaves. Mix well. Check the final seasoning. Add a touch of salt if necessary.
- To serve: Divide the fried rice into 4-6 portions and serve on individual serving dishes or in a large plate for family style dining. Sprinkle with crunchy dried shallots and garnish with fresh mint leaves. Serve hot.

Yellow rice

NASI KUNING

This really reminds me of my Grandmother's cooking - delicious yellow rice with lemon grass, lime leaves and coconut. Serve with fish, chicken or pork.

Serves 6-8

Ingredients:
- 300g uncooked white rice
- 1 stalk lemon grass, crushed
- 1 pandan leaf, torn into a few pieces
- 10cm fresh turmeric, peeled and grated or 2 tsp ground turmeric
- 50ml litres water
- 2 lime leaves
- 400ml coconut milk (or 200ml coconut milk and 200ml water for a lighter taste)
- 1 tsp of salt

Directions:
- Place the grated turmeric in water. Mix well and strain to make a turmeric extract. If you use ground turmeric, simply add water, mix well and set aside.
- Rinse the rice under running water and drain.
- Combine the coconut milk, rice, turmeric extract and salt in a pan, mixing well.
- Add the lemon grass, pandan and lime leaves.
- Cook the rice uncovered over a medium heat, until the water evaporates, stirring occasionally.
- Cover the pan, turn off the heat and let the rice sit for 20 minutes before serving.

Acehnese fried noodles with prawns and mixed vegetable

MIE ACEH

It is very easy to cook this as long as you have prepared all the ingredients beforehand. If you do not have leftover rice, use freshly cooked rice but let the rice completely cool to room temperature before cooking. The ginger gives a very delicious flavour and fragrance. No soya sauce required for this dish.

Ingredients
- 500gr fresh yellow noodles
- 12 medium prawns, peel and devein. (keep the tail intact)
- 400-500ml prawn stock
- 2 medium carrots, grated
- 50gr beansprout, roots removed
- 8 tbsp sweet soya sauce
- 3 tbsp salty soya sauce
- 200gr shallots, peeled and sliced thinly
- 2-3 tbsp coconut oil or vegetable oil
- salt to taste if necessary

For the Paste:
- 1 tbsp ground dried red chilli flakes
- 8cm each fresh ginger and turmeric
- 4 cloves of garlic
- 5 candlenuts
- 1 ½ tbsp curry powder (mixture of roasted ½ tsp each fennel, cumin, coriander seeds, cardamom, black pepper and fenugreek)

Other ingredients
- Sliced lime
- Shallots and cucumber pickles (optional)
- Melinjo nut crackers
- Deep-fried shallots (optional)

Directions:
- To make prawn stock, heat a pan and add 1 tbsp of oil. Cook the prawns until they turn a pink reddish colour (around 3-4 minutes). Add 1 litre water. Cook and reduce the liquid to half. Set aside.
- Grind the turmeric, ginger, garlic, candlenuts and chillies. Set aside.
- Heat a wok or a pan, add the oil and the sliced shallots. Cook until golden brown. Add the paste and cook for around 2-3 minutes. Add the curry powder. Cook for an extra a minute, stirring all the time.
- Add the stock and soya sauce. Add the prawns and cook 2-3 minutes. Check the taste. Add more salt if necessary.
- In the meantime, cook the noodles in boiling water for 2-3 minutes, strain and transfer into the sauce mixture with all the vegetables. Cook for another 2 minutes.
- Divide the noodles into four or six individual plates or serve it on a large serving plate to share. Add some raw grated carrots and beansprouts on top. Place the prawns on the side. Garnish with sliced lime and melinjo nuts on the side. Serve hot.

Meatballs with rice noodles

MIE BAKSO

This is one of the iconic Jakarta street foods served with a touch of vinegar to give a slightly sour flavour, plus sweet soya sauce and ground boiled chillies. The texture of the meatballs is firm, similar to typical Chinese fish balls.

Serves 4-6

For the Meat Balls:
- 500gr lean minced beef
- 100gr sago flour
- 50gr garlic, peeled and sautéd until golden brown. Set aside to cool and grind finely
- 2 tsp freshly ground white pepper
- 1 whole egg
- 50gr ice cubes

For the Beef Stock:
- 2 kg beef bones without fat
- 5 litres water

- 1 tbsp each of freshly ground nutmeg and white pepper
- 3 tbsp sea salt
- small bunch of celery sticks
- 50gr of garlic, peeled and sliced thinly

Other Ingredients:
- 200gr fresh or dried noodles
- Tomato sauce (optional)
- 50ml soya sauce
- 5 tbsp crunchy fried shallots (see page 38)
- Simple boiled chilli sambal (see page 36)
- 4 tbsp chopped celery leaves

Directions:
- To make the broth: put the beef bones and 2 litres of water in a stockpot and bring to the boil. Discard the water and rinse bones.
- Add 3 litres of water to the beef bone, together with the garlic, celery, salt, nutmeg and white pepper. Bring to the boil and simmer for 3-4 hours for a delicious stock.
- To make the meatballs: put all the meatball ingredients except the flour into a food processor and process until fine.
- Add the flour little by little while the food processer is on. Process until all the mixture has a smooth and silky texture.
- Transfer the mixture into a large bowl and form small balls. Simply add to the broth.
- Once the cooked meatballs float on the surface of the broth, turn the heat to low.
- In the meantime, cook the rice noodles according to the instructions of the packaging. Refresh with water, sieve and set aside.
- To serve: divide the noodles into four or six serving bowls. Add 3-4 meatballs and enough broth to each bowl and season with a touch of vinegar, tomato sauce, chilli sambal, sweet and salt soya sauce. Sprinkle with crunchy fried shallots and chopped celery leaves. Serve immediately.

Chicken noodles

MIE AYAM

Around every corner of the city streets you can find this dish – we call it Jakarta's noodle made by vendors individually for each customer – a ritual to be enjoyed. Mie Ayam is literally 'noodle chicken' a delightful infusion of galangal, lemongrass, sweet soya sauce, straw mushrooms, or the button variety if you prefer, in a steaming bowl of Chinese style wheat flour noodles. It can also be served with a clear chicken broth, which you sip separately or plunge it into your bowl. For extra flavor add some sambal.

Serves 4

Ingredients:
- 400gr fresh noodles or 300gr dried noodles (follow cooking instructions on the package)
- Large bunch of pak choy, chopped roughly
- 2 litres boiling water
- Garlic oil

For the garlic oil:
- 100ml coconut oil or vegetable oil
- 6 cloves garlic, peeled and finely chopped
- Salt and white pepper to season

For the chicken and mushroom mixture:
- 2 large chicken breast, sliced into cubes
- 100gr straw or button mushrooms, sliced around ¼ cm thickness
- 50gr shallots, peeled and sliced thinly
- 4 cloves of garlic, peeled and chopped finely
- 5cm galangal, peeled and sliced thinly
- 1 lemon grass stalk, crushed and tied into a knot
- 3 lime leaves
- 5 tbsp sweet soya sauce
- 2 salam leaves or bay leaves
- 1 tbsp regular soya sauce
- 3 tbsp coconut oil or vegetable oil
- 50ml water or chicken broth
- Salt and white pepper to season

Sambal (optional):
- 6 birds eye chilies, boiled for 5 minutes and ground finely with pestle and mortar
- 50ml water
- 1-2 tbsp of rice vinegar or white wine vinegar
- Salt to season

Other ingredients:
- Wonton skin, from an Asian grocery store, cut into triangles and deep fried

Directions:
- For the garlic oil, heat a frying pan, add the oil and garlic, and sauté for around 5 minutes and season with salt and white pepper. Set to aside to cool. You may keep and use the left over oil for a week.
- To make the sambal: mix the ground or chopped chillies thoroughly with water, vinegar and season with salt. Set aside.
- Heat the oil in a frying pan. Add the chicken cubes and cook until slightly golden brown. Transfer to a plate.
- Using the same plate, add one more tablespoon cooking oil, add the shallots and garlic, sauté for around 2-3 minutes, stirring all the time. Add the mushroom, lemon grass, sliced galangal, lime leaves, salam leaves and cook for around 3-4 minutes.
- Return chicken back into the pan and add water or chicken stock, soya sauce and cook for another 10 minutes over low heat to infuse all the ingredients. Season with salt and white pepper. Check the final seasoning and keep these ingredients warm.
- If you are using fresh noodles cook in boiling water for one minute (or follow instructions for packaged noodles).
- Divide the noodles into 4 pre-heated bowls.
- Add one-teaspoon garlic oil and mix well with chopsticks.
- In the meantime, add the pak choy into hot water, cook for 10 seconds and strain.
- Divide the vegetables into 4 portions and add on the side of the noodles.
- Top with 2 tablespoons or more of chicken mixture. Add one wonton cracker or pangsit and serve immediately, with sambal on the side if you wish.

Stir-fried noodles, chicken, eggs and sweet soya sauce

BAKMIE GORENG DENGAN AYAM, TELUR DAN KECAP MANIS

From street stalls to fine restaurants, this dish can be found everywhere in Jakarta and around the archipelago. The chicken and eggs can be replaced with seafood, tenderloin beef or pork.

Serves 4

Ingredients:
- 300g fresh or dried noodles (simply follow the cooking instructions on the packaging)
- 1 chicken breast, sliced into 1cm strips (season with salt, black pepper and 1 tbsp lime juice, 2 minutes before cooking)
- 5 shallots, thinly sliced
- 3 garlic cloves, crushed
- 2 red chillies, thinly sliced
- A handful of pak coy or any Asian green vegetable
- 2 spring onions, thinly sliced
- 2 eggs, beaten
- 2 tbsp coconut oil or vegetable oil
- 2 tbsp soy sauce
- 1-2 tbsp water
- Salt and black pepper

Directions:
- Heat the oil in a frying pan. Add the chicken strips and cook until slightly golden brown.
- Transfer to a plate.
- In the same frying pan, add the garlic and chillies, sauté for 2 minutes. Then add the eggs and cook for 30 seconds.
- Add the spring onions and vegetables, then immediately add the noodles and chicken and mix well.
- Add the soy sauce. Cook for 5-7 minutes over medium heat, making sure to stir the mixture frequently. If you find the mixture too dry, add 1-2 tbsp of water. Season with salt and black pepper and serve.

Laksa Medan

Traditionally asam gelugur or asam keping (the dried fruit of garcinia atrovirdis) is added to this dish to give an acidic flavour. I replaced it with tamarind for convenience, as it is not easy to buy asam gelugur. You may use any type of noodles. Here, I used dried kwetiau, a rice noodle which is similar in shape to linguine pasta.

Serves 4-6

For the fish Broth:
- 500gr or 1 whole ikan tenggiri (Spanish mackerel), filleted
- 1.5 litre water

For the Paste:
- 10 shallots, peeled and chopped roughly
- 4 garlic cloves; peeled and chopped roughly
- 6cm fresh ginger and turmeric; peeled and chopped roughly
- 2 lemon grass stalks, white part only, chopped finely
- 3 red curly chillies and 2 bird eye chillies (or your preference)
- 1 tsp shrimp paste or replaced with 2 tbsp fish sauce

Other Ingredients:
- 5 kecombrang (remove the outer layer and slice 2 pieces finely and 3 into halves)
- 3 lime leaves
- 1 tbsp sugar; salt to taste
- 2 tbsp coconut oil or vegetable oil
- 75gr tamarind pulp, soaked in 200ml hot water. Strain.
- a small bunch of kemangi (local basil) or mint leaves
- 200gr fresh or dried kwetiau, follow the cooking instruction on the package.

For Garnish:
- 2 red curly chillies, sliced thinly
- 3 shallots, peeled and chopped finely
- 2 small cucumbers, deseeded and chopped into small cubes
- a small bunch of basil or some mint leaves

Directions:
- Gut and clean the fish. Fillet the fish.
- Bring to the boil 1.5 litre water. Add the fish fillet and cook for 5-7 minutes. Remove the fish pieces and set aside.
- Put the head and bones of the fish into the hot water. In the meantime, remove the skin from the fish flesh. Shred and set aside.
- Add the fish skin and bones back to the stock and simmer for 45 minutes.
- In the meantime, grind well all the paste ingredients. Set aside.
- Heat a large pan. Add the oil and add the paste. Cook 3-4 minutes or until fragrant.
- Add the sliced kecombrang and sauté for a few seconds and add 1.2 litre fish stock and tamarind water. Add the halved kecombrang, kaffir lime leaves and small bunch of kemangi, sugar and season with salt. Add the shredded fish and simmer all the ingredients for 20 minutes. Check the final seasoning. You will have a rich fish broth with bursting with sweet, sour and some spicy flavours.
- To serve: prepare the kwetiau. Follow the packaging instruction for dried noodles from the package. For fresh kwetiau, simply divide the noodles into 4-6 individual serving bowls.
- Add the very hot broth, top with chopped cucumber. Sprinkle with sliced chillies, chopped shallots and garnish with mint or basil leaves. Serve immediately.

East Java clear spiced chicken soup

SOTO AYAM LAMONGAN

This is a truly a bowl of comfort. It has many surprising layers of flavours. In traditional way it is important to add koya which is a mixture of finely ground crunchy sliced garlic and shrimp crackers. If it is difficult to get shrimp crackers you may just add a touch of garlic powder. Add a touch of lime juice and sambal for more interesting flavours. In some regions of Indonesia, coconut milk is added into this soto.

Serves 6-8

For the Chicken broth:
- 1 whole large chicken, remove the skin and cut into 4 pieces
- 2 litres water
- 4 lemon grass, crushed
- 8 lime leaves, torn into halves
- 10 whole black pepper corns
- 5-7 red birds eye chillies, chopped into 3 pieces
- 2 spring onions and 2 of springs Chinese parsley, chopped roughly
- 20 shallots, peeled and chopped roughly

- 7 cloves of garlic, peeled and chopped roughly
- 10cm fresh ginger and turmeric, peeled and chopped thinly
- 5 candle nuts (kemiri), roasted and ground finely
- salt to season
- 50ml lime or lemon juice (add more if necessary)

Extra Ingredients to Serve in Individual Warm Serving Bowl:
- Use 20gr glass noodles per person. 120-160gr glass noodles, soaked in hot water, refreshed with cold water, strained and set aside

- 2 tbsp chopped Chinese celery
- 3 red tomatoes, deseeded and cut into small cubes
- 100gr beansprouts (discard the roots)
- 150gr white cabbage, sliced thinly
- 3 tbsp home-made crunchy deep-fried shallots;
- 5 eggs (perfectly boiled with the egg yolk cooked but still soft in the middle) – optional
- 3 tbsp koya (optional)
- 6-8 lime or lemon wedges extra if needed
- Boiled sambal (see page 36)

Directions:
- Put the chicken pieces into a large pan and add 2 litres of room temperature water.
- Add all the rest of the ingredients, except lime or lemon juice. Simmer for 1.5 hours to infuse all the herbs and spices.
- Turn down the heat to gentle and bring the stock to a simmer. Covered, for 1 hour.
- After half an hour, remove any scum that rises to the surface with a ladle.
- At the end of the cooking time, remove the chicken pieces from the broth. You may slice the chicken meat or pulled with using 2 forks.
- To serve, prepare all the individual bowls. Put a small portion of glass noodles (use a fork to create a glass noodle nest). Add the sliced cabbage, beansprouts, cubed tomatoes, sliced chicken or pulled chicken. Sprinkle with chopped Chinese celery, crunchy shallots and koya. Add half of the boiled eggs. Pour the very hot broth into the bowls. Serve immediately with sambal and extra lime wedges on the side.

Makassar beef soup with fermented soya

COTO MAKASSAR

Coto Makassar is a well-known soto from South Sulawesi. It includes many different spices and has been strongly influenced by Middle Eastern cuisine with the presence of cumin, coriander and cinnamon, and the addition of fermented soya beans, or tauco. Tauco is similar to miso in Japanese cuisine although more rustic in contrast to the smooth and fine texture of miso.

The mixture of spices, tauco, lime juice and chilli is a perfect combination. It is important to cook the beef slowly to achieve the desired tenderness. This soto is simply delicious and full of flavor.

Serves 10 as a Starter or 4 for a Full Meal with Plenty of Meat

Ingredients:
For the Coto:
- 1kg stewing beef, cut into cubes
- 1½kg beef bones
- 2 small sticks of cinnamon
- 4 lemon grass sticks, crushed and tied into a knot
- 5 kaffir lime leaves
- 3 tbsp of coconut oil or vegetable oil for sautéing the paste
- 2 litres of homemade stock (see beef stock directions)

- 75ml fresh lime juice
- 2 star anise
- 1 tsp cloves, roasted and ground
- Salt and black pepper to taste

For the Paste:
- 200gr of peeled and sliced shallots
- 7 roughly chopped cloves of garlic
- 50gr each of chopped galangal and ginger
- 50gr roasted and ground raw peanuts
- 1½ tbsp of whole coriander, roasted
- 1 tbsp of cumin, roasted

- 2 tbsp of tauco
- 5 red birds eye chillies
- 1 tbsp of palm sugar or brown sugar

Extra Ingredients for Serving:
- Sambal tauco (see recipe below)
- 2-3 thinly sliced spring onions
- 4 tbsp of deep-fried shallots
- Lime juice to taste

For the Tauco Sambal:
- 50gr red birds eye chilli
- 2 tbsp of tauco
- Juice of 2 limes
- 100ml water
- Salt to season
- ¼ tsp of sugar

Directions:
- First prepare the beef bones. Place in a large pot and add water to cover the bones. Bring to the boil and after 2-3 minutes, discard the water. Add around 3 litres water and bring to the boil.
- In the meantime, make the paste by simply grinding all the ingredients finely except the brown sugar, nuts and tauco. Use a pestle and mortar or a food processor.
- In a large frying pan, add cooking oil and the paste. Sauté for around 8-10 minutes on medium heat. Keep stirring.
- Add the beef cubes and cook until the meat has mixed well with the paste for around 10 minutes. Stir from time to time. Then add tauco, nuts and sugar, lemon grass and cinnamon stick. Sauté for 3-4 minutes. Transfer the mixture to the water and the bones, stir well. Bring to the boil and simmer for 2 hours,
- Simmer until the beef is tender and the broth is infused with all the ingredients. Add the lime juice and season with salt. Check the final taste.
- In the meantime, prepare the sambal. Simply boil the chilli then place into a bowl of cold water. Then grind the chilli and mix with the tauco, lime juice, water, salt and sugar.
- To serve: remove the bones. Divide the soup into 10 or 4 serving bowls and sprinkle with deep-fried shallots and sliced spring onions. Serve with extra sambal on the side.

Sour and spicy fish soup with pineapple

LEMPAH KUNING, SUP IKAN ASAM PEDAS DENGAN NANAS

This is from Bangka Island in Sumatera, the home of tin mining. Usually, mackerel is used but you may replace it with cod or any other white fish. The texture of the soup is watery with a beautiful infusion of fresh roots, spices, chillies and lemongrass. The freshness and acidity comes from a touch of tamarind and pineapple, which also gives it a sweet fragrance. You can add prawns and squid into this dish to make it a seafood soup. It has a delicious sour and spicy flavour.

Serves 4

Ingredients:

- 300g fillets of red snapper or any white fish, cut into 3cm wide pieces
- 1 small pineapple (225g)
- 2 red tomatoes, chopped roughly
- 1 litre of water
- 3 cloves of garlic, peeled and chopped thinly
- 50g shallots, peeled and chopped roughly
- 5gr each fresh ginger, turmeric and galangal, peeled and sliced thinly
- 3 red birdseye chillies, chopped roughly
- 2 stalks of lemon grass
- 1 tsp shrimp paste (roasted) or replaced with 1-2 tbsp of fish sauce
- 25gr tamarind pulp
- ½ tsp sugar
- Salt to season

Directions:

- Prepare the pineapple by peeling and removing the eyes. Cut half of the pineapple into bite sized pieces.
- Cut the lemon grass into 6cm lengths. Use the back of your knife to bruise them to release the flavour
- Pour water into a large pot. Add all the ingredients except sugar, salt and fish, bring to the boil and simmer for 20-30 minutes to infuse the flavours
- At this point, add the fish and cook for 1 or 2 minutes on low-medium heat and serve immediately. If you want to serve the soup in a contemporary way, strain the broth and put it back into the pan, reheat and add the sliced fish and cook for 1 or 2 minutes.
- Have four warmed soup bowls ready. Ladle the soup, along with the fillet of fish, into each bowl. Add some pineapple pieces. Sprinkle with small cubes of tomatoes and sliced thin chillies. Serve immediately.

Hot and sour prawn soup with asam sunti

SUP UDANG ASAM MANIS DENGAN ASAM SUNTI

It is important to have nice broth for this soup. I simply saute the paste with the prawn heads and shells in a little coconut oil or vegetable oil and add water to bring the flavour out.

Serves 4

Ingredients:
For the prawns:
- 800 gr medium-sized prawns (about five prawns for each person)
- Juice of 2 limes
- Salt and black pepper to season

For the Paste:
- 100 gr shallots, peeled and roughly chopped
- 4 garlic cloves, peeled and roughly chopped
- 10 cm fresh turmeric, peeled and roughly chopped, or 1 teaspoon turmeric powder
- 10 pieces asam sunti, roughly chopped, or 50 gr tamarind paste diluted in 100 ml water then strained
- 5 curly red chilies, roughly chopped
- 2 tbsp coconut oil or vegetable oil

For the Broth:
- Prawn heads and shells
- 5 fresh belimbing wuluh
- 4 large green chilies, sliced about 1 cm thick
- 4 lime leaves; 1 liter water.

To garnish:
- Round slices of belimbing wuluh and whole large green chilies

Directions:
- Clean the prawns, remove heads and shells and set aside, but leave tails intact. Make a slit on the back of each prawn to remove the vein.
- Roughly grind all the ingredients for the paste (except for the coconut oil or vegetable oil) with a mortar and pestle.
- Heat a large pan, add the coconut oil or vegetable oil and saute the paste for about 2 to 3 minutes. Add the prawn shells and heads and saute for another 2 minutes, always stirring.
- Add a liter of water, along with rest of the ingredients for the broth. Bring water to the boil and simmer for about 15 minutes. Season with salt and black pepper.
- Strain the soup, return liquid to the pot and reheat over a low flame.
- In the meantime, season the prawns with salt and black pepper and add lime juice. Marinate for 2 minutes, then add the prawns to the soup and cook for about 3 to 4 minutes.
- Divide the soup into four bowls, garnishing each with sliced belimbing wuluh and a whole green chili. Serve the soup hot by itself or with a bowl of rice.

Salad and Savoury Combinations

Corn cakes with tomato salsa

PERKEDEL JAGUNG DAN DABU-DABU

The humble corn is revitalized with lime leaves.

Serves 4

Ingredients:
- 4 corn cobs or 250g of tinned corn in water
- 2 cloves of garlic, crushed and finely ground
- 5 shallots, finely sliced
- 3 fresh lime leaves, finely sliced
- 1 whole egg plus 1 egg white
- 3 tbsp corn flour
- 5 tbsp plain flour
- 3 tbsp finely chopped spring onion
- Salt and black pepper to taste
- Coconut oil or vegetable oil for deep frying
- Tomato salsa (*dabu-dabu*, see page 35)

Directions:
- Slice the corn from the cob and pulse in a food processor for one minute. The texture will be a mix of fine and rough. Transfer the corn into a large bowl
- Add the garlic, shallots, lime leaves, and spring onions and mix well
- Stir in both flours
- Add the eggs and seasoning and mix well until you have a thick batter
- Heat the oil in a frying pan.
- Using two spoons, scoop together a tbsp-sized portion of the batter and carefully drop it into the hot oil. Useful hint: use one spoon to scoop the batter and the second spoon to help scrape the batter into the hot oil.
- Deep fry until golden brown.
- Transfer the corn cakes onto a kitchen towel to absorb the excess oil.
- Serve with tomato salsa.

Mixed vegetable salad with spice and zingy peanut sauce

LOTEK

Lotek is similar to gado-gado, karedok or pecel. Each of them can be different in how the vegetables are served: raw or cooked; with the addition of kencur (aromatic ginger); with or without peanut sauce. In the classic recipe, the vegetables are cooked but I prefer to serve some vegetables raw and to roast rather than deep-fry the peanuts to maintain their natural goodness.

This is a dish best served chilled, to enjoy its refreshing taste of light, elegant spice and the zing from the peanut sauce. I have substituted baby spinach for water spinach and red cabbage instead of white cabbage to produce a more vibrant colour. If it is difficult to buy snake beans, use French beans instead.

Serves 4-6

Ingredients:
- 2 medium carrots, peeled: use a potato peeler to make ribbons
- 2 medium cucumbers, peeled, halved, de-seeded and prepared in the same way as the carrots
- 50gr young snake beans or French beans; blanched and sliced into 1cm lengths
- 30gr beansprouts roots, discarded; washed and dried
- 100gr red or white cabbage, the tougher outer layer discarded, washed, dried and sliced thinly
- 30gr baby spinach, washed and dried with a kitchen towel.

For the dressing:
- 1 clove of garlic, peeled
- 3cm aromatic ginger (alternatively use 5cm ginger but you will not smell the distinctive aroma and taste of aromatic ginger)
- 2-3 red curly chillies
- 20gr tbsp palm sugar
- 1½ tbsp lime juice
- 125ml water
- 75gr roasted peanuts

Directions:
- To roast the peanuts simply place on a baking tray in a pre-heated oven at 150°C. Roast for around 10 minutes or place in a frying pan (no oil) and cook over a low-medium heat for around 10 minutes, stirring from time to time
- Prepare the vegetables and place in the refrigerator to chill.
- To make the dressing, simply grind the garlic, aromatic ginger and chillies until fine. Then add the peanuts and grind finely.
- Place the peanut mixture into a bowl and add the rest of the ingredients. Mix well. The texture of the sauce should be creamy but not too thick.
- Take the bowl of vegetables from the refrigerator. Add half of the dried shallots and toss in the dressing.
- Divide the mixture into four serving plates and garnish with the rest of the crunchy shallots. Or serve a large serving plate family style. Serve immediately.

This salad can be enjoyed on its own or with cold cuts of meat or chicken.

Mini savoury minced beef omelette with pastry

MARTABAK ASIN

This is one of the most well known dishes among Jakarta street foods. Martabak has a crunchy texture, with minced beef and herbs inside. The unique cooking technique requires the thin pastry placed in hot oil in a flat large pan, with the egg mixture added. I have chosen to adapt the recipe by using ready-made spring roll pastry and to use a standard frying pan. Serve with shallots, cucumber and pickled green chillies. It is perfect for a snack or a starter with simple mixed salad.

To Make 6 Mini Martabak:

- 20 small springroll pastry or dumpling pastry (store-bought and ready to use)
- 200gr lean minced beef
- 4 cloves of garlic, peeled, grated or finely chopped
- 30gr spring onions, sliced thinly
- 2 small onions, peeled and finely chopped
- 2 tbsp coconut oil or vegetable oil
- Salt and fresh black pepper to taste
- 2 whole eggs
- 2 egg whites, lightly beaten
- 200ml coconut oil or vegetable oil for frying
- Pickled cucumber, shallots and green chillies (see page 37)

Directions:

- Heat a frying pan and add 2 tbsp coconut oil or vegetable oil. Add the chopped onions and garlic and sauté over a low-medium heat for around 10 minutes.
- Add the minced beef and spring onions. Cook for another 10 minutes and stir from time to time.
- Season with salt and black pepper and set aside to cool.
- Add 2 eggs and mix well.
- Take one sheet of pastry and add 1 heaped tbsp of the cooked beef mixture. Brush the pastry edges with egg white and cover with one extra sheet. Repeat until all mixture is used.
- Heat a frying pan and add oil until hot. Place one piece of martabak, cook until golden brown. Turn it over until done. Repeat with the rest of the martabak.
- Put martabak on a flat plate with a paper towel to absorb excess oil.
- Divide the martabak into 2 pieces. Serve hot with pickled chillies, cucumbers and shallots.

Manadonese Risotto

TINUTUAN, BUBUR MANADO

This dish is normally eaten for breakfast as a porridge in Manado. I like to serve it as main dish for lunch or dinner as a risotto, baking the pumpkin and sweet potatoes first.

Serves 4

Ingredients:
- 300g round grain white rice, preferably risotto rice
- 200g pumpkin, peeled, deseeded, the fibre removed and cut into large chunks
- 200g sweet potatoes, peeled and cut into large chunks
- 2 fresh cobs of corn, kernels sliced off the cob or 200g canned corn
- 200g water spinach or spinach
- 1 litre hot water
- 2 stalks lemon grass, crushed
- A handful of basil
- 4 garlic cloves, crushed
- 10 shallots, thinly sliced
- 4 tbsp coconut oil or vegetable oil
- Salt and black pepper to taste
- Cooked prawns (optional)

Directions:
- Pre-heat the oven to 180°C or gas mark 4.
- Place the pumpkin and sweet potatoes in an ovenproof dish. Season with salt, black pepper and 2 tbsp of oil. Cook until soft and set aside.
- Heat the oil in a large frying pan. Add the shallots and garlic, sauté for 3 minutes.
- Add the rice, turn off the heat and stir until the rice is totally coated.
- Turn the heat back on, add the lemon grass and 3 ladles of hot water (or just enough to cover the rice). Simmer, stirring until the rice has absorbed nearly all of the liquid. Continue to add stock as the existing stock is absorbed. After about 17 minutes the rice is nearly cooked.
- Add the cooked pumpkin, sweet potatoes and corn. Mix well and cook for 5 minutes. Add more stock if necessary, to make sure the rice has a creamy consistency.
- Add the spinach and basil, cook for 2 minutes.
- Season with salt and black pepper. Serve.

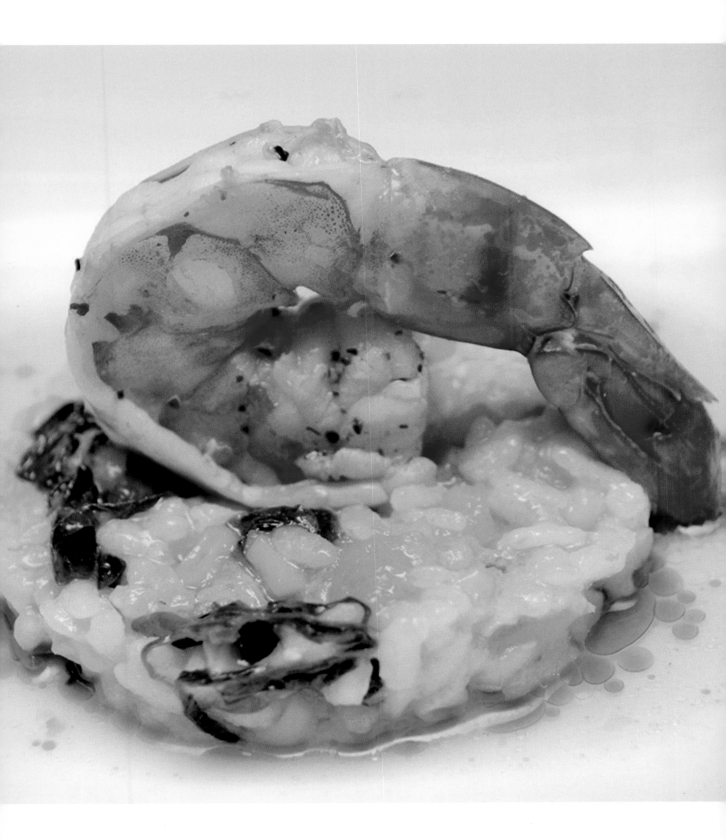

Mixed vegetable curry

SAYUR LODEH

This is a very mild curry, flavoured with fresh lemon grass and basil.

Serves 4-6

- 1 large chayote, washed, cut into 2cm cubes and put into a bowl with cold water
- 200g eggplant, washed, cut into 3cm cubes and seasoned with salt to reduce bitterness
- 300g pumpkin or butternut squash, deseeded, peeled and cut into 2cm cubes
- 2 garlic cloves, crushed

- 3 chillies, thinly sliced
- 5 shallots, peeled and thinly sliced
- 5cm ginger, peeled and finely chopped
- 1 lemon grass, crushed
- A handful of basil
- 500ml water or vegetable stock (see page 38)
- 250ml thick coconut cream
- 2 tbsp coconut oil or vegetable oil
- Salt and black pepper to taste

Directions:
- Heat the oil in a pan. Add the shallots, garlic, chillies and ginger. Cook for a few minutes until fragrant.
- Cook the pumpkin, eggplant and lemon grass for 5 minutes. Stir from time to time.
- Add the chayote and water or stock, season with salt and black pepper.
- Simmer for 15-20 minutes or until all vegetables are soft but still retain their shape.
- Add the coconut cream and basil. Simmer for another 5 minutes.
- Season with salt and black pepper and serve.

Urap

URAP

Urap is a classic Sundanese vegetable dish with many different vegetables mixed with a spiced coconut dressing and kencur, a type of aromatic ginger. It adds new layers of flavors to the urap and you may add roasted pumpkin for a different texture.

Serves 8

For the Urap:
- 100gr baby carrots, peeled and grated
- 50gr long beans
- 100gr red cabbage, thinly sliced
- 100gr beansprouts, with sprouts removed
- 50gr horenso or Japanese spinach, with stems removed
- small bunch of basil or kemangi , with stems removed

For the Paste:
- 75gr shallots, peeled
- 2 cloves garlic, peeled
- 4 curly red chilli peppers or more for a spicier taste
- half tsp roasted shrimp paste or 1 tbsp fish sauce
- 5cm aromatic ginger/kencur; half tbsp sugar
- half tsp lime juice
- 3 bay leaves
- 2 tbsp coconut oil or vegetable oil
- half a fresh coconut flesh, finely grated and seasoned with salt (make sure the coconut is not too young, when the flesh is soft, or too old, when the flesh gets hard)

Making the Urap:
- Blanch the long beans whole in boiling water, then take out immediately and douse with ice water.
- Chop the beans into half-centimeter segments. Set aside.
- Keep all the vegetables in the refrigerator until ready to use.

Making the Coconut Dressing:
- Finely grind all the paste ingredients except the bay leaves and coconut.
- Heat a frying pan over medium heat and add 2 tbsp of coconut oil orvegetable oil.
- Sauté the paste and bay leaves for about 4 to 6 minutes until fragrant. Transfer the mixture into a bowl to cool.
- Add the grated coconut to the spice mixture and steam for around 10 minutes.
- Steam the long beans separately for 3 to 4 minutes.
- Remove the long beans from the steamer and put into a bowl with ice water to stop the cooking process. Set aside.
- Remove the coconut and paste mixture from the steamer.
- Add the sugar and season with salt. Check the seasoning. Set aside to cool. Discard the bay leaves.
- To serve, simply mix all the vegetables, basil and the coconut mixture.

Roasted eggplants with chillies

TERONG PANGGANG BALADO

A well-known West Sumatra vegetable dish, Terong panggang balado is traditionally deep fried, but I have chosen to roast the vegetables. Serve with steamed white or yellow rice as a good accompaniment to beef rendang, any curry dish or even a simple mixed salad for a lighter meal.

Serves 4

Ingredients:
- 3 large purple eggplants
- 50ml olive oil, vegetable oil or coconut oil
- 2 tbsp salt to season

For the Chilli Paste:
- 50gr shallots, peeled and thinly sliced
- 3-4 red bird's eye chillies, finely ground
- 2 cloves garlic, peeled and thinly sliced or finely ground
- 3 large red tomatoes, cut into medium cubes
- 2 tbsp cooking oil
- Salt to season
- A few kemangi leaves for garnish

Directions:
- Cut the eggplants into 2-centimeter length. Season with salt and leave for around 20 minutes in a colander.
- Pre-heat an oven to 180° Celsius. Pat the eggplants dry, toss them into a little vegetable oil and place them on a baking tray. Roast them for about 20 minutes until tender. Remove from the oven and set aside to cool.
- To make the chilli paste: heat a frying pan and add 2 tablespoons of oil. Add the shallots and garlic and cook for 2-3 minutes. Add the finely ground chillies and cook for another 2 minutes. Stir throughout.
- Add the chopped tomatoes and cook for around 5 minutes. Season with salt.
- Add the roasted eggplants to the tomato and chilli paste mixture. Cook for 3-4 minutes. Check the seasoning.
- To serve, divide the eggplant balado onto four serving dishes, sprinkle with kemangi leaves and serve immediately with a small bowl of steamed rice.

Mixed Raw Vegetables with Sambal Terasi

LALAPAN SAMBAL TERASI

One of the most popular sambals in Indonesia, traditionally the terasi or shrimp paste is overwhelmingly the dominant element. However by adding just a little touch of terasi, this sambal gains a wonderfully savoury flavour. Also popular in Malaysia, where it is known as "belacan" the popularity of sambal terasi is similar to that of fish sauce in Thai cooking, or bonito flakes in Japanese cuisine. As an option try 1 or 2 finely ground anchovies instead of shrimp.

Ingredients:
- 4 small carrots, washed, peeled and cut into halves
- 3 medium cucumbers, washed in mineral water, quartered
- Romaine salad leaves (optional)
- Small white cabbage, washed and cut into small wedges
- 2 tomatoes cut into wedges (optional)
- A small bunch of long beans (snake beans) or baby French beans, washed and dried
- A small bunch local basil, washed and dried

For the sambal:
- 6 shallots, peeled and chopped roughly
- 1 clove of garlic, peeled and chopped roughly
- 3 curly red chillies
- 2 tomatoes, halved
- ¼ tsp shrimp paste (you can buy ready-to-use shrimp paste at the supermarket or replace with 1-2 pieces of anchovies).
- 1 tbsp vegetable oil or coconut oil
- 1-2 tbsp lime juice
- Salt to taste (don't add salt if you are using anchovies)

Directions:
- Prepare the vegetables and set aside. Put in the refrigerator
- Heat a frying pan. Add the oil
- Add the shallots, garlic, and chillies and cook for 1 minute
- Add the shrimp paste and cook for 15 seconds; add the tomatoes and cook for another 45 seconds. Turn the heat off. Remove the tomato and chop roughly.
- Using a pestle and mortar, finely grind the shallots, garlic and chillies. Add the shrimp paste and grind further. Add the chopped tomatoes and continue grinding.
- Season with salt and lime juice
- Transfer the mixture into a small bowl, and the dish is ready to be served with a mix of the raw vegetables.

Twice cooked Tofu soya cake with tamarind and coriander

TAHU TEMPE BACEM

It has interesting sweet taste from coconut water and palm sugar with a touch of tangy flavour from the tamarind. You may enjoy this dish as is or add it to a simple mixed salad or serve with steamed rice and stir fried vegetables

Serves 10

- 10 small square tofu around 1.5cm x 1.5cm
- 200gr soya cake, cut into 10 square pieces around 1.5cm x 1.5cm
- 5 tablespoons sweet soya sauce
- 30gr tamarind paste
- 500ml coconut water
- 2 tablespoons palm sugar or brown sugar
- 50ml vegetable oil
- Salt to season

Paste:
- 50gr shallots, peeled and roughly chopped
- 5 cloves of garlic, peeled and roughly chopped
- 1 tablespoon coriander seeds, roasted and ground finely

Directions:
- Ground finely the shallots, garlic, and coriander seeds. Transfer into a medium pan and add the sugar and mixed well.
- Add the coconut water, soya sauce and tamarind paste and mixed well.
- Make slit the top of tempe and tofu and add into the liquid mixture. Season with salt and cook until the liquid evaporated.
- Heat a large frying pan and add vegetable oil and add several tempe and tofu and brown both side of tempe and tofu which takes around 2-3 minutes each side. Continue to brown all the tempe and tofu until all browned. Serve warm immediately.

Fried Tempe and Tofu

TEMPE AND TAHU GORENG

I must include *tempe* and *tahu goreng* although I can understand that it is still difficult to buy tempe outside Indonesia but tofu is mostly available. This combination is perhaps the king of Jakarta street foods. It is on every corner of the city. The key to a delicious *tempe* and *tahu goreng* is a mixture of garlic, shallots, coriander and salt to marinate the *tempe* or tofu before deep-frying. Enjoy it with green chillies and simple *sambal kecap*, a mixture of choped green chilli and sweet soya sauce. You may cut the *tempe* thick for a moist and juicy result or extra thin for a crunchy texture. I really like to add them both to a mixed green salad to give extra layers of flavours and texture.

Serves 10

- 10 small square *tempe* and tofu, 2 x 2cm thickness
- 100gr tempe, sliced thinly
- Salt to season
- Vegetable oil for deep-frying
- Some fresh green chillies (optional)

Paste:
- 50gr shallots, peeled and roughly chopped
- 5 cloves of garlic, peeled and roughly chopped
- 1 tablespoons coriancer seeds, roasted and ground finely
- 100ml water
- Salt to taste

Directions:
- Ground the shallots, cloves and coriander seeds finely.
- Into a large mixing bowl, mix the paste with with 100ml water and season with salt
- Add the tempe and tofu, and marinated for around 10 minutes.
- Heat a frying pan and add plenty of oil and deep fried the tempe and tofu until golden brown.
- Place the temple and tofu on a plate with kitchen towel to absorb excess oil and transfer them into a serving plate and serve immediately.

Meat and Poultry

West Sumatera dried beef curry

RENDANG

A dried beef curry from West Sumatera, this is one of Indonesia's most popular dishes. Rendang is easy to find along any food street in Jakarta and certainly at any Padang restaurant. It takes time to make - around 5-6 hours - until the coconut cream with spices is completely absorbed to create a rustic extract with a delightful dried and caramelized texture. It is important to use thick coconut cream to stay loyal to the authentic recipe. Or you can add desiccated coconut for even better results and coconut milk which is normally more available in supermarkets. Serve with steamed rice.

Serves 10-12 People

Ingredients:
- 1½ kg topside beef, cut into 4cm pieces
- 1½ litres thick coconut milk
- 5 kaffir lime leaves
- 1 turmeric leaf (optional), chopped roughly
- 2 salam leaves or bay leaves
- 10gr tamarind paste (dilute with 100ml coconut cream, squeezed, mixed well and strained)

Paste:
- 100gr shallots, peeled
- 5 cloves of garlic
- 50gr curly red chillies
- 10gr red birds eye chillies
- 20gr fresh ginger, peeled
- 30gr fresh galangal, peeled

Directions:
- In a large pan or wok, mix coconut milk with the paste, lime leaves, turmeric leaf and bay leaves. Cook for around 10 minutes to infuse the flavour and warm the coconut.
- Add the desiccated coconut and the meat, bring to the boil and cook for around 5 minutes. Season with salt.
- Turn the heat to low and cook for around 3 hours, until the meat is tender.
- Now turn up the heat, cooking until the mixture dries and turns a dark brown. Taste and add a touch of salt if necessary.
- Serve with steamed rice. To create Nasi Padang serve rendang accompanied by several other dishes.

Acehnese duck curry

SIE ITIK, GULAI BEBEK ACEH

This is the perfect dish for a rainy day. You can serve it with brown rice and sautéd French beans and corn kernels with garlic, shallots, lemon grass and lime leaves. Feel free to replace with your favorite vegetables.

Serves 4-6

Ingredients
For the duck:
- 1 whole duck, cut into 6 pieces
- salt and black pepper to season
- 2 tbsp lime juice
- 1 stick cinnamon
- 2 white cardamom pods
- 2 lemon grass stalks, crushed
- 1 pandan leaf, roughly chopped
- 100ml tamarind water
- 3 star anise
- 200ml coconut cream
- 100ml water
- 2 tbsp coconut oil or vegetable oil

For the Spices:
- 1 tsp whole coriander seeds
- half tsp whole cloves
- half tsp whole black peppercorns
- half tsp cumin
- half tsp fennel
- 4 candlenuts

For the Chilli Paste:
- 10 large dried red chilli peppers
- 3cm fresh ginger, peeled and roughly chopped
- 50gr shallots, peeled and roughly chopped
- 3 cloves garlic, peeled and roughly chopped

Directions:
- Prepare the tamarind water: soak 30gr of tamarind paste in 150ml water for 10 minutes. Mix well and strain. Set aside.
- Prepare the chilli paste: soak the dried chilli peppers in hot water until soft. Roast the dried spices in a pan without oil for 3 to 4 minutes, then grind and set aside.
- Remove the chilli peppers from the water and finely chop and grind together with the shallots, garlic and ginger. Set aside.
- Clean the 6 pieces of duck. Season with salt, black pepper and lime juice. Set aside.
- Heat a frying pan and add the oil. Add the chilli paste and cook for 4 to 5 minutes, stirring constantly. Add the dried spices and mix well.
- Add the duck and mix well before adding the tamarind water and bringing to a simmer.
- Add the lemon grass and lime leaves. Season with salt and black pepper and cook on low heat for 2 hours.

Slow-cooked beef with caramelized shallots and spices

SEMUR MANADO

This is another dish which features the influence of Arabic and Chinese cooking, mixed spices and sweet soya sauce which create the unique Indonesian flavour. This is a really comforting beef stew and it is a perfect meal for a big crowd.

Ingredients:
- 1 kg beef suitable for stew, cut into 3 cm pieces
- 100 gr plain flour
- 3 tbsp coconut oil or vegetable oil
- 6 cloves of garlic
- 250 gr shallots, peeled
- 6-7 tbsp sweet soy sauce
- 2 tbsp lime juice (optional)
- 1 tbsp ground cloves, black pepper and nutmeg powder
- 1½ litres of water or homemade beef stock
- Salt to taste

Directions:
- Dry the beef with a kitchen towel and season with salt and black pepper. Coat each piece in flour, patting off the excess.
- Heat a frying pan, add 2 tbsp of oil and brown the beef chunks for 1 to 2 minutes on each side. Set aside.
- Heat a new pan. Sauté half the shallots for 1 minute, add the garlic and sauté until golden brown,
- Add the beef, mix well and add the water or stock.
- Add the soy sauce and all spices. Simmer for 2 hours or until the beef is very tender. Add the rest of the shallots after one and a half hours.
- Taste the stew when the beef is tender. Cook until the texture of the sauce is creamy, and some of the shallots tender but still whole.
- Add salt and black pepper to taste.

Beef croquettes with simple salad

KROKET

This dish is influenced from Dutch cooking. You can buy croquettes everywhere around the city. To make something more interesting I serve the croquettes with a simple mixed salad which is a perfect light meal. Serve with fresh green chillies the classic way or with mustard sauce.

Serves 6

Ingredients :
- 500gr leftover or freshly cooked potatoes, mashed finely
- 200gr minced beef
- 3 cloves of garlic, peeled and finely chopped
- 3 eggs
- 1 tsp freshly grated nutmeg
- 1 tbsp of olive oil
- 50gr of butter
- Salt and black pepper to taste
- 100gr flour
- 150gr breadcrumbs
- 100gr oatmeal
- 1 litre oil for deep-frying

For Mustard Sauce:
- 1 tsp mustard
- 2 tbsp mayonnaise.

For the Salad:
- Small bunch of Romano or other salad leaves
- 3 tomatoes sliced into wedges
- Small bunch of fresh basil (optional)

For the Dressing:
- 4 tbsp extra virgin olive oil
- 2 tbsp lime juice
- Salt and black pepper to taste

Directions:
- For the croquettes; mash the leftover or freshly boiled potatoes using a ricer if you have one, or a fork. Set aside.
- Heat a frying pan. Add a tbsp of oil and 20gr of butter. Add the garlic, cook until slightly golden, then add the minced beef and cook for around 5-6 minutes until brown. Season with salt and black pepper, set aside to cool.
- Lightly beat one of the eggs and add to the mash along with the cooked minced beef, including the juice and melted butter, grated nutmeg, salt and black pepper to taste. Mix well.
- Place the flour and breadcrumbs in separate bowls. Beat the remaining two eggs in a fourth bowl.
- Take small handfuls of the potato mixture and shape into logs or cylinders of around 10cm length. Roll each in flour, dip in the beaten egg and coat in breadcrumbs, then dip in egg again and coat with oatmeal. Repeat until all the mixture is used. Place the croquettes in the fridge to chill for 30 minutes.
- For deep-frying, fill a large saucepan with 1 litre oil on medium heat. Make sure the oil is hot before frying the croquettes in batches, turning occasionally until they are golden brown. Place the croquettes on a paper towel lined plate.
- In the meantime mix the mustard and mayonnaise. Set aside and keep in the refrigerator.
- Mix all the salad ingredients. Set aside.
- To serve: divide the salad mixture between 6 different serving plates adding two croquettes each. Add a tsp of mustard and mayonnaise mixture or 2 fresh green chillies. Drizzle the salad with the dressing. Serve immediately.

Beef stew with carrots and potatoes

EMPAL GENTONG DENGAN WORTEL DAN KENTANG

This is a well-known dish from the West Java, Purwakarta area. Rice is a common side item to this soupy dish, but I add carrots and potatoes instead to give it a splash of colour, while also presenting a full meal in one pot. Dried powdered chillies are also a customary ingredient in empal gentong but I have chosen to use freshly chopped chillies. Traditionally empal gentong contains offal but I only use meat for this recipe.

Serves 8-10 People

Ingredients:
- 1 kg of stewing beef, cut into 4cm cubes
- 3 lemon grass stalks, crushed and tied into a knot
- 4 lime leaves
- 2 salam or bay leaves
- 250ml of coconut milk
- 2 tbsp coconut oil or vegetable oil
- 300gr potatoes, peeled and cut into cubes
- 200gr carrots, peeled and cut into chunky 1.5cm pieces
- juice of 1 or 2 limes (optional); salt and black pepper to season
- 1.5-2 litres of hot water or home made beef stock

For the Paste:
- 100gr of shallots, peeled. 50gr whole and 50gr sliced thinly
- 4 cloves of garlic, peeled and sliced thinly
- 4 candlenuts, roasted and chopped roughly (8 macadamia nuts can be used as an alternative)
- 6 cm of fresh turmeric, roasted, or 1 tsp of turmeric powder
- 3cm of galangal, peeled and chopped thinly
- 4 whole cloves
- 1 tsp of salt

To Garnish:
- A small bunch of chives, sliced thinly
- 3 curly chillies or 6 red birds eye chillies for a more spicy flavor, sliced thinly
- 2 tbsp of crunchy deep-fried shallots

Directions:
- Grind the cloves, half of the shallots, garlic, candlenuts and fresh turmeric with a pestle and mortar. Add a touch of salt to make it easy to grind. Set aside.
- Heat the clay pot with a medium flame and add coconut oil or vegetable oil. Add the paste and cook for around 3-4 minutes.
- Meanwhile, season the meat with salt and black pepper and add it into the paste mixture. Cook until the meat changes color to a lighter brown.
- Add lemon grass, bay leaves, lime leaves. Add half of the hot beef stock or water and cook in low-medium heat for 2 hours. Add some hot water from time to time.
- After two hours add the potato cubes, carrots and whole shallots. Pour in the rest of the stock or water and cook until the vegetables and potatoes are tender. This will take around 30 minutes in low-medium heat.
- Add the coconut milk and season with salt and black pepper. Check the final seasoning. Cook for an extra 5 minutes before serving the soup in individual bowls.
- Finally, add the chopped chives, chopped chillies and crunchy shallots.

Aromatic white chicken curry

OPOR AYAM

There are many different styles of opor ayam around Indonesia. This version has a more Sumatera flavour with many different varieties of spices. For simple varieties you can omit the clove, nutmeg and cinnamon. It gives a lighter flavour but is still really delicious.

Ingredients:
- 6 chicken legs (around 800 gr)
- Juice of 1 lime
- ½ heaped tsp of salt
- ½ heaped tsp of black pepper
- ½ heaped tsp of clove powder
- ½ heaped tsp of freshly grated nutmeg
- 2 sticks of cinnamon
- 2 lemon grass stalks, crushed and knotted
- 2 kaffir lime leaves
- 2 salam leaves (local bay leaf)
- 1 tbsp palm sugar

- 2 tbsp coconut oil or vegetable oil
- 350 ml water
- 150 ml coconut cream
- Salt and black pepper to taste

For the Paste:
- 3 cloves garlic, peeled and roughly sliced
- 100 gr of shallots
- 8 cm of ginger and 8 cm of galangal
- add 1 tbsp of coriander seeds, roasted and ground
- 2 candlenuts, ground

Directions:
- Season the chicken portions with salt, black pepper and lime juice and mix well. Set aside.
- To prepare the paste, simply grind the garlic, shallots, ginger and galangal with a pestle and mortar into a fine texture.
- Heat a frying pan. Add the oil and the paste, cooking for two minutes before adding the coriander seeds, candlenuts, clove powder, nutmeg powder and cinnamon sticks, and cook for a further 30 seconds.
- Add the lemon grass, lime and salam leaves, cook for a few seconds.
- Add the water and simmer for 5 minutes to infuse all the spices and herbs.
- Add the chicken and cook for 8 to 10 minutes on low to medium heat. Add the coconut cream. Season with salt and black pepper and cook for another 5 minutes. You will have a creamy sauce with perfectly cooked, tender chicken.
- Serve with steamed white or brown rice or boiled potatoes with green vegetables.

Acehnese fried chicken with curry, lime and pandan leaves

AYAM TANGKAP

This dish is fun as a finger food. It is twice cooked chicken, simmered with plenty of spices and deep-fried with infused pandanus and curry leaves. The mixture of spices, shallots, garlic, tamarind and infused leaves makes this a delicious meal.

Serves 10
Two drumsticks per person

Ingredients:
- 20 chicken drumsticks
- 200ml water
- 50gr tamarind paste
- Salt and black pepper to taste
- Large bunch of curry leaves
- 10 pandan leaves, chopped into 3 cm strips
- 20 lime leaves
- Coconut oil or vegetable oil for deep-frying

For the Marinade:
- 150 gr shallots, peeled and sliced finely
- 4 cloves of garlic, peeled and chopped finely
- 75 gr fresh ginger
- 50 gr of peeled galangal
- 10 gr of peeled turmeric and 5 birdseye chillies, chopped roughly

Directions:
- Season the chicken drumsticks with salt and black pepper.
- Chop the ginger, turmeric and galangal finely, then add the chillies and grind together with a pestle and mortar. Mix with the chopped shallots, garlic and turmeric. Add this paste to the chicken together with the ground fresh spices. Make sure the drumsticks are coated in the mixture, then transfer to a large pot.
- Mix the tamarind and water, squeezing the tamarind to extract its flavour. Strain and add the water to the pot.
- Bring the chicken and tamarind water to the boil, then cook on a low-medium heat for around 45 minutes.
- Heat a large wok or frying pan and add the coconut oil or vegetable oil. Make sure the oil is hot before adding the chicken. Add the pandan, curry and lime leaves 5 minutes later. Fry the chicken until slightly golden.
- Transfer the fried chicken and leaves onto a large plate lined with kitchen towel to absorb excess oil. Then serve immediately.

Roasted chicken, Lombok style

AYAM TALIWANG

Roast chicken has universal appeal as a powerful comfort food. Those sharp popping sounds from the oven and the wondrous aroma that fills the kitchen build anticipation and appetite. One of the key ingredients in this dish is kencur, or aromatic ginger. It is not easy to find outside of Indonesia, but it can be replaced with double or triple the amount of regular ginger. This dish serves four.

Ingredients:

- 1 whole chicken, weighing about 1.5 kg
- 2 tbsp coconut oil or vegetable oil
- 2 tbsp lime juice
- 3 red tomatoes, finely chopped
- 1 tsp palm sugar or brown sugar
- salt and black pepper

For the Paste:

- 125 gr (around 14 bulbs) shallots, peeled and thinly sliced
- 4 garlic cloves, peeled and thinly sliced
- 5 cm kencur, peeled and thinly sliced
- 8 curly red chillies and 3-4 red bird's-eye chillies (optional)
- 1 tsp roasted shrimp paste, or 2-3 tbsp fish sauce

Directions:

- Preheat oven to 200°C.
- Cut along the backbone of the chicken with kitchen scissors or a sharp knife, then press firmly on the breastbone to flatten it. Wipe with a kitchen towel to dry the chicken. Set aside.
- Put all of the paste ingredients into a blender, or grind with a pestle and mortar until fine.
- Heat the oil in a frying pan, add the paste and cook for 4-5 minutes until the mixture is a little bit dry. In the meantime, season the chicken with salt, black pepper, oil and lime juice. Set aside.
- Add tomatoes and cook for another 4-5 minutes, or until the texture resembles that of thick sambal. Keep stirring over low heat
- Add sugar and lime juice. Season with salt and black pepper. Mix well and taste the seasoning. Set aside to cool for 5-7 minutes.
- Prick the chicken with a sharp knife and smear the paste all over it. Leave it to marinate in the refrigerator for more than an hour in a large dish.
- Remove the chicken from the refrigerator 30 minutes before cooking.
- Put the chicken in a baking dish with baking paper and pour the leftover paste on top. Cook for about 50-60 minutes. Serve with steamed brown rice and stir-fried vegetables or sautéed potatoes and salad.

Chicken curry with pineapple

KARI AYAM NANAS, PALEMBANG

There are many tropical fruits you can add to curry-mangosteen, hairy lychee, mango or pineapple – to give it a fruity and light flavour. For this recipe, I use skinless chicken drumsticks. Drumsticks afford more flavour than any other part, but you need to allow lots of time to prepare it. If you are pressed for time, you can replace the drumsticks with chicken breasts.

Serves 8Ω

Ingredients:
- 16 chicken drumsticks, skinless
- Juice of 2 limes
- 1 pineapple – remove the skin and eyes and dice into cubes
- Salt and black pepper to taste

For the Paste:
- 6 red birds-eye chillies, soaked in hot water until soft
- 10 shallots, peeled
- 2 cloves of garlic, peeled
- 5 cm galangal, roughly chopped
- 10 cm fresh turmeric, peeled
- 2 tbsp fish sauce or 1 tsp dried shrimp paste
- 1 tbsp freshly ground coriander
- 2 candle nuts
- 2 lemon grass roots, crushed
- 2 kaffir lime leaves
- 1 tsp sugar
- 225 ml thick coconut cream
- 500 ml hot water
- Fresh coriander leaves for garnich

Directions:
- Grind the chillies, shallots, candle nuts, garlic and turmeric into a fine paste using a mortar and pestle.
- Heat a work or pan. Add 2 tablespoons of oil, add the paste and cook over low-medium heat for around 5 minutes until fragrant.
- In the meantime, season the chicken with salt, black pepper and lime juice, then add to the paste mixture. Add the rest of the ingredients except the water, pineapple and coconut cream.
- Simmer for around 45 minutes or 1 hour until the the chicken is thoroughly cooked and tender.
- Add the pineapple and the coconut cream and simmer for 5-7 minutes. If the mixture is too dry, you can add a little water to make sure that there is enough sauce.
- Taste the seasoning. Discard the lemongrass and lime leaves and garnish with coriander leaves. Serve with steamed rice and stir fried vegetables.

Goat curry with natural yoghurt

KARI KAMBING MEDAN

Originating from Medan in North Sumatera this goat curry can be served as indicated, with coconut milk, or you can try natural yoghourt instead. If you are not keen on goat it is fine to substitute beef, fish, chicken, tofu, tempeh or vegetables, especially pumpkin with carrots and French beans or long beans. This recipe is easy to make and for a big crowd, simply double or triple the ingredients. Serve with basmati rice. Add finely chopped fresh lime leaves for garnish and fragrance.

Serves 6-8

Ingredients:
- 1kg goat meat for stewing, season with salt and black pepper
- 2 lemon grass stalks
- 4 lime leaves
- 2-3 tbsp of coconut oil or vegetable oil
- 500 ml water
- 500ml coconut milk
- 5 fresh lime leaves, sliced finely
- 4-6 star anise to garnish
- Salt to season

For the Paste:
- 75 gr shallots, peeled
- 5 cloves of garlic
- 5 curly red chillies
- 5 red birds eye chillies (optional)
- 7gr fresh ginger and turmeric, peeled
- 4 candlenuts

For Dry Spices:
- 1 tsp each of coriander seeds, cumin, fennel seeds
- 6 cloves
- 4 white cardamoms (replaced with green cardamom if the white is not available)
- 2 star anise
- 1 tsp freshly ground nutmeg
- 1 tbsp freshly ground black pepper

Directions:
- Place all the dry spices (except the nutmeg) in a frying pan without oil. Cook the spices on medium heat for around 8-10 minutes or until fragrant. Grind all the spices except the star anise and cardamom. Roughly crush the cardamom and set aside.
- To make the paste, roughly cut all the ingredients and grind into a fine paste with a pestle and mortar or use a food processor. When using a food processor, the texture of the paste will be rough, not fine. Transfer the paste into a small bowl and set aside.
- Heat a large pan and add the cooking oil and then the paste. Cook the paste for 6-8 minutes, stirring all the time.
- Add the dry spices and then the beef. Let it cook for 5 minutes and mix well. Add the whole star anise and crushed cardamom. Add the water, bring to the boil and simmer over a very slow heat for 3-4 hours. Season with salt and check the seasoning.
- Add the coconut milk, stir the mixture well and cook for 5 minutes on a low medium heat. Check the final seasoning and transfer the curry into a large serving plate and serve hot. Garnish with finely sliced lime leaves and star anise. Sprinkle with some roasted cashew to give a crunchy texture to the dish.

Black nut beef stew

RAWON SURABAYA

Black nuts are known as buah kluwak. It is an important ingredient in sop konro, a hearty Makassar, South Sulawesi soup and also rawon, a hearty East Java soup served with steamed rice. Kluwak is also used in gabus pucung, a fish stew of Betawi cuisine. The recipe has the delicious flavours of lemon grass, chillies, ginger, turmeric, lime leaves and earthy kluwak. It is perfect to serve with rice cake or mashed potatoes. Make this stew one day before, keep it in the refrigerator and re-heat. It is perfect for a dinner party with a big crowd.

Serves 6-8

- 1.2kg sliced beef shank; salt and black pepper to season
- 3 tbsp coconut or vegetable oil
- 50gr beansprouts (short ones), washed and strained
- 1 spring onion, chopped finely
- 2 red curly chillies for garnish and 2-3 slices of limes
- Juice of 2 limes; emping crackers (optional)

For the Paste:
- 100gr shallots, peeled
- 4 cloves of garlic, peeled
- 1 tbsp coriander seed, pan roasted and ground
- 7 red birds eye chillies, chopped roughly (add more if you like a very spicy taste)
- 3 candlenuts
- 10cm each fresh ginger and turmeric - peeled and ground
- 2 lemon grass stalks, crushed
- 3 lime leaves
- 7 black nuts
- 1 litre homemade beef stock or water
- 2 tbsp coconut or vegetable oil
- Salt and black pepper to taste

Directions:
- To prepare the black nut: clean and brush each of the nut. Steam for 1 hour to soften the shell, or soak overnight. Crack the shell, remove the flesh and grind until fine. Set aside.
- Grind the chillies, ginger, turmeric, galangal and candlenuts until fine. Set aside.
- Cut the beef in large pieces around 2 x 2cm. Season the beef with salt and black pepper.
- To brown the meat: heat a frying pan and add 3 tablespoon coconut oil or vegetable oil. Place few slices of the meat and cook for 1-2 minute each side or until brown. Continue until all the beef is browned. Set aside.
- To make the rawon sauce:
  Heat a pan and add 2 tbsp coconut oil or vegetable oil using medium heat. Add the shallots and garlic, sauté for 2-3 minutes and add the ground paste mixture. Cook for another 4-5 minutes. Add lime leaves, lemon grass, black nut and the beef. Mix well.
- Add the beef stock or water, season with salt and black pepper and bring to the boil. Simmer for two hours or until the beef is very tender.
- Add the lime juice and continue to cook in medium-high heat to reduce the sauce until you have a thick texture. Check the final taste.
- To serve: transfer all the mixture into one large serving bowl. Sprinkle the beansprouts and finely chopped spring onion and garnish with whole red curly chillies. Serve with hot steamed rice or rice cake.

Chicken pop, cooked in coconut water with a modern bun twist

BURGER AYAM POP, PADANG

Before coconut water became the drink of sport fanatics and health conscious people around the world, coconut water has been a traditional drink for Indonesians for centuries, including its universal use for cooking. This burger is delicious with your favourite mixed salad.

Serves 6

Ingredients:
- 1 whole chicken around 1.2kg, cut into 4 pieces, skin discarded
- juice of 2 limes
- 4 lime leaves
- 2 lemon grass stalks, crushed
- 1 litre coconut water
- Salt

For the Paste:
- 50gr shallots, peeled
- 3 cloves of garlic, peeled

- 5 cm fresh ginger and galangal; peeled
- 1 tbsp whole coriander seeds, roasted
- 2 candlenuts (or replaced with macadamia nuts)
- ½ tsp whole white pepper, roasted
- 1 tsp salt

For the Sambal:
- 50gr shallots, peeled and sliced thinly
- 2 cloves garlic
- 5 red birds eye chillies
- 5 papaya chillies (large chillies)

- 3 large tomatoes (lightly score the base of each tomato with a cross)
- 3 tbsp lime juice
- 3 tbsp coconut oil or vegetable oil for sautéing
- 1 tsp sugar
- Salt to taste
- 500ml water for boiling

Other Ingredients:
- 6 medium burger buns, 50gr mixed salad leaves and roasted paprika or sliced tomatoes and your favourite salad dressing

Directions:
- For the paste, grind all the ingredients finely.
- Season the chicken with salt and add the lime juice. Rub the paste into the chicken all over and marinate for around one hour.
- Pour the coconut water into a large pan and add the chicken and lime leaves, lemon grass and salam leaves and bring to the boil. Simmer for around 1 ½ -2 hours until very tender.
- In the meantime, prepare the sambal. Bring to the boil half a litre of water and add the all the ingredients except the lime juice. Cook the tomatoes for 3-4 minutes, remove and skin them. Cook the rest for around 10 minutes. Take all the ingredients, chop and grind finely with pestle and mortar. Transfer the mixture into a bowl, season with salt and lime juice. Set aside.
- Slice each of the buns into half and warm them on the griddle pan. In the meantime, remove the chicken pieces from the pan and place on a large plate. Use two forks to pull the flesh from the bones. Mix the chicken with the sambal and add 2-3 tbsp of the leftover boiled coconut water to give moisture into the chicken and sambal. Check the final taste. Add salt and a touch of lime juice if necessary.
- Divide the chicken into 4 portions. Place mixed salad leaves on the base of the hot-griddled bun and add the chicken. Top with the other half of the bun and serve immediately with a small portion of your favourite salad and dressing.

Sate: Indonesia's favourite – and probably the food dish most associated worldwide with our archipelago of flavours. Not surprisingly there are local and regional variations, each claiming to be unique and of course most are represented on the streets of the capital city of Jakarta. Sate may consist of sliced, diced or minced chicken, beef, pork, goat, or seafood. Meat is marinated or mixed with spices and herbs, skewered, barbecued and served with or without sauce. You can make Indonesian sate at your own home with the flavour of Bali, Madura, Padang (West Sumatera), Manado, North Sumatera – or why not invent your own local variation? Experiment and enjoy!

Sate Republic

Minced seafood sate from Bali

SATE LILIT DARI BALI

This is very exotic using lemon grass stalks as skewers offering many delicous layers of flavours. You can use the seafood mixture to make fish cakes.

Serves 4

Ingredients:
- 300 gr white snapper skinless fillet (any fillet of white fish can be used)
- 300 gr prawn, discard shells and heads
- 3 tbsp fresh finely grated coconut or 2 tbsp desiccated coconut
- 4 fresh lime leaves, sliced thinly
- Salt and black pepper to season

Ingredients for the Paste:
- 10 shallots, peeled
- 4 cloves of garlic, peeled
- 4 curly red chillies
- 7cm fresh ginger, peeled
- 7cm fresh turmeric, peeled
- 7cm fresh galangal, peeled
- (alternatively 1 tsp each of ginger, turmeric and galangal powder)
- 1 tsp freshly ground black pepper
- 1 tsp coriander seeds, roasted and ground.
- 3 stalks of lemon grass, finely chopped, using only the white part
- 2 tbsp of tamarind paste, seeds removed
- 1 tbsp palm sugar or brown sugar
- 2 candlenuts or replaced with 4 macadamia nuts
- Salt to season

Directions:
- To make the paste: put the chopped shallots, garlic, chillies and root spices into a food processor to create a fine paste, or grind with a pestle and mortar. Transfer the paste into a bowl and set aside.
- Chop the fish fillets and prawns roughly and process in the food processor to a fine consistency. Transfer the mixture into a large bowl and season with salt and black pepper. Add the sliced lime leaves and grated coconut and mix well.
- Take a tbsp of the mixture and mold using your hand onto a lemon grass stalk to create a uniform thickness - an elongated drumstick leaving enough stalk for the handle. Repeat until all the mixture is finished.
- Brush each of the sate with oil and barbecue over hot charcoal or place under a pre-heated griller and rotate them from time to time to cook them evenly until brown. This will take around 10 minutes under a grill. Serve hot with urap or a simple mixed green salad with lime dressing.

Classic chicken satay with a peanut and lime sauce

SATE AYAM DENGAN SAUS KACANG DAN AIR JERUK

Adding a tangy flavour to the classic Indonesia satay.

Serves 6-8

- 6 chicken thighs deboned and cut into small bite-sized cubes
- 1 tsp salt
- 1 tsp black pepper
- 2 tbsp lime juice
- 2 tbsp sweet soya sauce
- 1 tbsp coconut oil or vegetable oil
- Bamboo skewers (soaked in water for 1 hour to prevent burning)

Satay Sauce:
- 2 chillies, thinly sliced (use more for a spicier dish)
- 1 tbsp sweet soya sauce
- 4 heaped tbsp crunchy peanut butter
- 50 ml tamarind water
- ½-1 tsp salt

For the Chicken:
- Mix all the ingredients in a bowl and marinate for 30 minutes.
- Thread 3-4 pieces of chicken onto each bamboo skewer. Repeat until all the chicken is used.
- Grill over charcoal for 3-4 minutes on each side, brushing the satay with any excess marinade as they cook. Turn over from time to time.
- Serve with the peanut sauce on the side and steamed rice.

For the Satay Sauce:
- Mix all the sauce ingredients in a bowl.
- For a creamier sauce, add more water.
- Season with salt and serve.

Goat sate Tanah Abang

SATE KAMBING TANAH ABANG

Goat sate is usually served with bigger pieces of meat than other types of sate. The additional sweet soya sauce with sliced chillies is special. You can substitute lamb if you like.

For 20 Skewers

Ingredients:
- 1kg tender goat meat, cut into cubes
- Season with salt and black pepper

For Marinade:
- 125ml sweet soya sauce
- 25ml lime juice
- 50 gr shallots, peeled and chopped finely
- 5 lime leaves, hard stems in the middle removed, sliced thinly and chopped finely

- 3 tbsp vegetables oil
- Salt and freshly ground black pepper to taste

Soya and Chillies Sambal:
- 60gr shallots, peeled and chopped finely
- 5-10 red or green birds eye chillies sliced thinly
- 100 ml sweet soya sauce
- 40-50 ml lime juice
- 3 red tomatoes, seeds discarded and cut into small cubes
- 3-4 tbsp crunchy deep fried shallots (optional – see page 38)

Directions:
- In a large bowl, mix all the ingredients for the marinade except the oil. Set aside.
- Season the goat meat with salt and black pepper and mix well. Add the marinade and keep in the fridge for one hour.
- In the meantime, soak the sate skewers in water to prevent them burning during barbecuing. Also prepare the charcoal and the fire.
- After one hour, insert 4 pieces of meat into each of the sate skewers and repeat until all the meat is finished. Keep the marinade mixture.
- Brush each sate with oil and place on the hot barbecue.
- Keep turning the sate sticks to make sure they do not burn or overcook.
- From time to time, brush the sates with left over marinade and oil and continue until the meat is cooked thoroughly – about 8-10 minutes.
- Place the sates on a serving plate with the soya and chilli sambal on the side.
- Enjoy as is or with steamed rice or compressed lontong rice and some stir-fried vegetables.

Pork satay with chilli and ginger paste

SATE BABI RICA-RICA DARI MANADO

Gingery and tangy flavours are dominant in this satay. The pork can be replaced with filleted white fish, prawns or chicken.

Serves 4

- 400g pork fillet, cut into bite-sized cubes
- Bamboo skewers (soaked in water for 1 hour to prevent the skewers from burning)
- 2 tbsp lime juice
- 1 tsp salt

Paste:

- 2 garlic cloves, peeled and roughly chopped
- 10cm ginger, peeled and roughly chopped
- 10 shallots, peeled and roughly chopped
- 10 chillies
- 2 tbsp lime juice
- 2 tbsp coconut oil or vegetable oil
- Salt to taste

Directions:

- Put all the paste ingredients, except the lime and oil into a blender, or grind with a pestle and mortar to make a fine paste. Season with salt and lime juice, and add the oil. Mix well.
- Season the pork with lime juice, salt and add the paste. Mix well and marinate for 10 minutes.
- Thread 3-4 pieces of pork onto each bamboo skewer. Repeat until all the pork is used.
- Grill over charcoal for 4-5 minutes each side, sprinkling the satay with any excess marinated as they cook. Turn over from time to time.
- Serve with steamed rice.

Beef sate Padang with spices

SATE PADANG

Classic sate Padang normally uses beef and offal such as liver and heart. The beef and offal normally are boiled first with many different spices, herbs and oil until tender, sliced into small pieces, skewered then barbecued. The stock is used to make the sauce, thickened with rice flour. I have simplified by using beef tenderloin only and have made the sauce with classic spices and plenty of shallots for thickening the sauce. Cook the sate over a hot grill, barbecue or over a hot griddle pan. Sate Padang has a vibrant curry flavour from the cumin, chillies and turmeric.

Makes Around 10-12 Skewers

Ingredients:
- 400gr tenderloin beef, cut into small cubes
- 1 tsp roasted cumin
- 2 tbsp coconut oil or vegetable oil
- Salt and freshly ground black pepper to season

For the Sauce:
- 200gr shallots (around 30), peeled and sliced thinly (50gr for deep-frying shallots)
- 3 cloves of garlic, peeled and chopped finely
- 8 curly red chillies, ground
- 5cm fresh ginger roots, peeled and grated
- 10cm fresh turmeric, peeled and grated or 1 tsp turmeric powder
- 1 tbsp roasted coriander seeds, ground
- 1 tsp roasted cumin, ground
- 2 sticks of lemon grass, crushed
- 5cm fresh galangal, peeled and grated
- 500 ml water or homemade beef stock
- 250ml coconut oil or vegetable oil for deep frying the shallots
- Salt and black pepper to season

Cooking Directions:
- To prepare the fried shallots. Heat a frying pan and the oil. Season a quarter of the sliced shallots with salt and fry until golden brown. Remove and place on a paper towel to absorb excess oil. Set aside.
- To make the sauce: heat a frying pan, add 2 tbsp of coconut oil or vegetable oil, the shallots and garlic, and cook until soft and brown. You will find the mixture becomes dry. Keep stirring from time to time. Add the chillies and the rest of the ingredients, except the water. Cook for another 5 minutes in low heat.
- Add the water, bring to the boil and simmer for 20 minutes. Season with salt and black pepper.
- Discard the lemon grass and put the mixture into a food processor. Process till silky smooth for 2-3 minutes. Transfer into a pan and set aside.
- To cook the sate: Season the beef with cumin, salt and black pepper. Then drizzle with coconut oil or vegetable oil and mix.
- Thread 4-5 pieces of beef onto each bamboo skewer.
- Place the beef sate on a griddle pan and let it cook for 2-3 minutes each side.
- In the meantime, reheat the sauce. Pour it over the cooked sate, add a sprinkle of crunchy fried shallots. Serve with steamed white or brown rice.

Sweet and aromatic beef sate maranggi from West Java

SATE MARANGGI

This sate combines the flavours from the spices with a touch of sweetness from palm sugar and sweet soya sauce. You may use brown or coconut sugar instead of palm sugar and there is no need to add any sauce. After marinating, you can barbecue or cook the beef in a griddle pan. It is nice to cook the beef "medium well" a little pink in the middle but please do not overcook or the meat will become rubbery and tough.

Ingredients:
- 400gr beef tenderloin, cut into small cubes
- 2 tbsp sweet soya sauce
- 2 tbsp coconut oil or vegetable oil
- 1½ tbsp lime juice
- 2 tbsp palm sugar
- 1 tbsp ground coriander seeds
- Juice of 1 lime
- Salt and black pepper to taste
- 12-bamboo skewers (to serve as canapés you'll need 24 mini bamboo skewers)

Paste:
- 2 tbsp coriander seeds, roasted and ground
- 50 gr shallots, peeled and sliced thinly
- 1 clove of garlic
- 3-4 birds eye chillies, sliced thinly (add more chillies if you wish)
- 3 cm aromatic ginger (kencur) optional, peeled and sliced thinly
- 6 cm fresh ginger, peeled and sliced thinly
- 2 lemon grass stalks, use the white part only, sliced thinly

Directions:
- To prepare the paste. Grind all the ingredients except the palm sugar with pestle and mortar.
- Mix the soya sauce, lime, palm sugar, oil and coriander seeds into a large bowl. Add the meat and the paste and marinate for 1 hour in the refrigerator.
- Heat a frying pan; add 2 tbsp of oil and sauté the paste for around 5 minutes over a low-medium heat. The texture will be dry.
- Add the paste into the marinade mixture and mix well. Set aside.
- To prepare the sate. Place 4-5 pieces of beef onto each bamboo skewer.
- Place the beef on a very hot griddle pan or barbecue for one minute each side. Brush the meat with the left over marinade and cook for 1-2 more minutes each side. Serve hot.

Juices, Sweets and Drinks

Carrot, pineapple and ginger juice

JUS WORTEL, NANAS DAN JAHE

A very refreshing drink.

Serves 1-2

- ½ pineapple, peeled
- 2 apples
- 2 medium size carrots, peeled
- 10cm (1 thumb) fresh root ginger, peeled

Directions:
- Cut the pineapple, carrots and ginger into rough chunks and put them through a juice extractor.
- Keep in the refrigerator for one hour before serving or add a few cubes of ice although the flavour will dilute a little bit after adding the ice cubes.

Soursop juice

JUS SIRSAK

This milk-coloured juice is so refreshing! Just add a touch of sugar to make it perfect.

Serves 4

- 200g soursop fruit, peeled; skin and seeds discarded, frozen
- 300ml low fat milk
- 4 tbsp sugar or 2 tbsp honey
- Plenty of ice cubes

Directions:
- Put all the ingredients in a blender until smooth.
- Divide the mixture into 4 serving glasses.

Mango juice

JUS MANGGA

Mango has sweet and aromatic taste.
Add some ginger and lime juice for
extra kick.
Serves 2

- 1 large mango, *harum manis, frozen*
- 3 tbsp lime juice
- 600ml ice water
- 15cm fresh ginger root, peeled

Directions:
- Put the fresh ginger root through a juice extractor. Set aside.
- Peel the mangoes and chop roughly. Then place in the freezer.
- Blend the mango, lime juice and ginger extract until you have fine mixture.
- Serve with long wedges of mango.

Ginger tea

WEDANG JAHE

Wedang jahe is infusion of fresh roots ginger, lemon grass and pandan leaves with water. Barbecue the ginger first to give it a smoky flavor, but this is an option. Add sugar syrup or palm sugar syrup for a touch of sweetness. Normally served in a large glass I like the idea to serve it in a teapot with proper teacups. This is a perfect tea for winter or a rainy day.

Serves 6-8 People

Ingredients:
- 100gr fresh ginger roots, brush the skin, no need to peel and roughly cut and crush to release the ginger oil
- 1 litre water
- 2 lemon grass stalks, crushed and tied into a knot
- 2 pandan leaves, chopped roughly, optional
- ½ tsp of salt (optional)

For palm sugar syrup: see page 39

Directions:
- Put water in a medium pan and add crushed ginger, lemon grass and pandan leaves, bring to the boil, turn the heat down low and simmer for around 20-25 minutes.
- In the meantime, prepare the sugar syrup.
- When the tea is infused, strain the tea into a teapot and it is ready to serve with sugar or palm sugar syrup or coconut sugar with your favourite biscuits or cake.

Rice pannacota with palm sugar syrup and cashew

BUBUR SUMSUM

This Javanese dish is the perfect dessert for those who prefer to avoid dairy and gluten. It has a similarly light and silky texture as Italian Pannacota with a delicious mixture of coconut flavour with the natural sweetness and caramel of palm sugar. To give this pudding more texture I added roasted, roughly ground cashews. However, you may replace these with *kacang kenari* (canarium nuts), local almonds or regular almonds.

Serves 12 in individual glasses

Ingredients:
- 100gr any brand or type of rice flour
- 1 litre of coconut milk, either homemade or store-bought coconut milk
- 1 tsp of salt
- 6 pandan leaves, tied into a knot
- 100gr cashew, roasted

For the Homemade Coconut Milk:
- 2 mature coconuts
- 1.5 litres of warm water or 1 litre tinned coconut milk

For the Palm Sugar Syrup:
- 200gr Coconut sugar
- 150ml of water
- 2 pandan leaves, tied into a knot

Directions:
- Pre-heat the oven to 180°C.
- Place the cashew nuts on a baking tray and put it in the oven. Bake for around 20-25 minutes or until they turn lightly golden. As an alternative, you can use a frying pan without oil. Heat the pan above a small-medium heat for around 10-12 minutes until lightly golden. Set aside to cool.
- Ground the cashews roughly with a pestle and mortar; set aside.
- To make the homemade coconut milk: remove the skin from the coconut; pour out the water then cut the coconut into four even pieces; grate the meat finely. If you have a strong blender, cut the coconut into small pieces blitz.
- Mix the grated coconut with warm water and squeeze the mixture over a sieve — your homemade coconut milk is ready.
- In a large saucepan, mix the rice flour with the coconut milk little by little and mix well. Add more coconut milk, salt and pandan leaves. Mix well.
- Heat the pan and whisk the mixture from time to time. The mixture will get thicker and creamier as it gets hot. Whisk continuously for around 12-15 minutes above a small-medium heat until you get a smooth, silky creamy texture as custard.
- Prepare 12 small glasses and pour an equal amount of the mixture in each. Set them a side to cool and place them in the refrigerator to chill for at least three hours or preferably over night.
- To prepare the palm sugar syrup: place the sugar in a medium pan; add water and pandan leaves.
- Heat the pan in slow-medium heat; let the palm sugar melt and form a syrupy texture. This will take around 5-7 minutes. When it cools, the liquid will get thicker. Set aside.
- Remove the chilled pannacota from the refrigerator, drizzle each glass with half or a tbsp of palm sugar syrup and sprinkle with ground cashew. Serve immediately.

Green pancakes with coconut

KUE DADAR GULUNG

The green colour of these pancakes comes from pandan leaf extract or use green food colouring if you wish. The pandan extract provides a beautiful fragrance.

Serves 6-8

Pancakes:
- 100g plain sifted flour
- ½ tsp salt
- 1 egg, lightly beaten
- 200ml full cream (you can use low fat milk)
- 50ml pandan leaf extract (see page 39)
- 25g butter, melted and cooled
- Coconut oil or vegetable oil for frying

Filling:
- 200g freshly grated coconut
- 150ml palm sugar syrup (see page 39)
- 2 cinnamon sticks
- ½ tsp salt

Directions:
- First make the filling. Place all the ingredients for the filling into a pan and heat over a medium heat for 5 minutes. Turn the heat to low and cook for 20 minutes more, stirring all the time. Set aside.
- Mix all the dry ingredients for the pancakes in a bowl. Add the beaten egg, then the butter, and slowly add the milk, continuing to hand whisk so that the mixture is not lumpy.
- Add the pandan leaf extract and stir. The mixture should now have a silky smooth texture.
- Transfer the mixture into a jug to make it easier to pour into a frying pan later on.
- Heat a non-stick pancake pan or frying pan. Add a few drops of coconut oil or vegetable oil and pour the pancake mixture (around 35-45ml) into the pan, spreading the mixture out to ensure the pancake is thin. Cook over a moderate heat for about one minute until set and golden-brown.
- Flip and cook for another minute.
- To serve the pancake warm, add the filling very quickly. Put 2 tbsp of the sweet coconut mixture on the pancake edge then roll it up. Slice the roll in two and serve immediately.

Coconut tart

KLAPPERTAART

A fusion of young coconut, custard, raisins and cinnamon. It is another culinary legacy from the Dutch for the people in Manado, North Sulawesi

Serves 8-10

Ingredients:
- 2-3 whole young coconuts, with the flesh scooped out
- 1 kg canned young coconut, drained
- 100gr raisins
- 100gr kenari nuts or almond flakes
- 200ml full cream milk
- 2 egg yolks
- 50gr sugar
- 1 tbsp corn flour
- 2 tbsp dark rum
- 5 tbsp condensed milk
- 1 tbsp cinnamon powder
- 5 cloves and 1 cinnamon stick
- 1 vanilla pod de-seeded (keep both seeds and pod)

Directions:
- Boil the cloves and cinnamon stick in 100ml water. Add the raisins and cook for 10 minutes.
- Remove the cloves and cinnamon stick, drain the raisins and leave to cool.
- Pre-heat the oven to 180°C or gas mark 4.
- Beat the egg yolks, sugar and corn flour in a bowl until creamy.
- Slowly heat the milk, add the vanilla seeds and pod to the saucepan and bring to the boil.
- Slowly pour the warm milk into the egg mixture, stirring constantly.
- Pour the custard mixture back into the pan, add the cream and condensed milk and stir over a low heat until the mixture thickens sufficiently to coat the back of a wooden spoon. Take the pan off the heat and add the rum.
- Put the coconut flesh and raisins into an oven proof dish and spoon the custard on top.
- Sprinkle with nuts and cinnamon and bake for 45 minutes until the top is brown.

Thick pancakes

MARTABAK MANIS

Pancake lovers, rejoice at this recipe which delivers a thick, honeycomb texture. The mixture of chocolate sprinkles, cheese, sesame seeds and condensed milk is rich but delicious - an occasional indulgence.

You will need a 15cm diameter metal frying pan

Serves 10-12

For the Thick Pancakes:
- 500gr flour
- 1 vanilla pod
- 1 tsp of baking powder
- 50gr sugar
- 2 eggs, lightly beaten
- ½ tsp of salt
- 650ml low-fat milk
- An extra tsp of baking powder

For the Topping:
- 30gr-salted butter
- 1 tsp of sugar
- 2 tbsp chocolate sprinkles
- 1 tsp of roasted white sesame seeds
- 30gr grated cheddar cheese
- 1 tsp of condensed milk (optional)

Directions:
- Cut the vanilla pod in half lengthwise, scrape out the seeds with the back of a spoon and set aside.
- Sift the flour and baking powder together into a large mixing bowl. Add sugar and mix well.
- Add the milk, little by little and mix by hand gently or use an electric hand mixture on slow speed until the mixture becomes silky smooth.
- Measure out 125gr of the mixture (that's about half a cup). Add ¼ tsp baking powder and mix well.
- Heat the frying pan over a medium heat then pour the mixture into the pan and cook for 2-3 minutes, until you have small bubbles appear, then turn the heat down low.
- Sprinkle each pancake with sugar, cover the pan and let it cook thoroughly until you can see a little hole opening on the top of each pancake.
- Remove and place on wooden board. You can now spread with the topping according to your preference; butter, chocolate sprinkles or shavings or Nutella spread, roasted white sesame seeds, grated cheese and an optional drizzle of condensed milk.
- Cut the pancakes into 10-12 halves and serve hot.

Coconut crème brûlée

KUE LUMPUR

Whether Kue Lumpur is the Indonesian version of the classic French Crème Brûlée is a matter of opinion. A more dense texture is evident with additional flour and mashed potatoes, which can be substituted with sweet potatoes. By using less amounts of flour and sweet potatoes, a lighter texture can be achieved.

Makes 10 Cakes

You'll need a pan with 6 small molds or you can use muffin tins and bake in the oven with 180°C for around 8-10 minutes.

Ingredients:
- 100gr flour, sieved
- 100gr pumpkin or sweet potatoes, banana – puree after steaming
- 500ml coconut cream

- 6 whole eggs
- 150gr palm sugar
- 1 tsp cinnamon powder
- 1 vanilla pods
- ½ tsp salt

Palm Sugar Syrup and Coconut Sauce:
- 150gr palm sugar or coconut sugar
- 100gr coconut cream
- 1 tsp cinnamon powder

Directions:
- Cut the vanilla pod in half lengthwise, scrape out the seeds with the back of a spoon and set aside.
- In a large bowl, add the eggs, sugar, salt, cinnamon and vanilla and beat with an electric hand mixer for around 8-10 minutes.
- Add the sweet potatoes or pumpkin puree, add the flour little by little, and beat at a slow speed until a silky batter is achieved.
- Add the coconut milk a little at a time to make sure there are no lumps in the mixture. Strain if necessary.
- Put the special mold pan on low-medium heat and brush with butter. When the pan is hot, pour the batter into the mold and cook for around 2-3 minutes. Remove and place on a plate. Repeat until all the batter is finished.
- To make the sauce, simply mix all the ingredients over low heat, until a caramel texture is achieved.
- Place one or two of the kue lumpur on individual serving dishes, drizzle with the sauce and serve immediately.

Sweet mashed cassava with grated coconut

GETUK LINDRI

This snack is a combination of mashed or finely ground cassava, sugar and freshly grated coconut. Sold on the streets in many different colours, white, yellow, green, chocolate and pink it is a commingling of soft silky textures and taste. I prefer natural rather than commercial food colouring, by using chocolate, pandan leaf extract or beetroot extract. It's important to use coconut that is neither too old, nor very young, in order to obtain the right level of moistness. You may substitute sweet potatoes for the cassava without needing to add any sugar.

Makes 16 Portions

- 500gr butter cassava with yellowish coloured flesh
- 125gr sugar
- 2 vanilla sticks
- 125gr grated coconut
- 1 tsp of pandan leaf extract
- 1 tsp of beetroot extract
- 1 tbsp of cocoa powder
- 1 tsp of salt (divided into 4 for serving)

Directions:
- Peel the cassava, cut into chunks and steam until soft.
- In the meantime, grate the coconut and prepare the vanilla sticks.
- Cut the vanilla sticks into halves lengthwise, using the back of the spoon to scrape out the seeds. Set the seeds a side. Keep the vanilla sticks or place them into a sugar jar.
- When the cassava is soft, remove from the steamer and transfer to a food processor, add sugar and process until soft and silky.
- Add half of the coconut and process for few seconds.
- Divide the mixture into 4 portions the vanillaseeds and add each of the colours – chocolate, pandan leaf and beetroot extract and mix each well adding a ¼ tsp salt to each. Leave one portion without any colour.
- Take scoops of the coloured mashed cassava and shape into spheres, using two spoons, until all the mashed cassava has been used up.
- Serve sprinkled with grated coconut as a snack any time or dessert.

Banana fritters

PISANG GORENG

There are many varieties of local banana in different flavours and sizes suitable for frying such as plantain, kapuk banana, ambon (similar to Cavendish) king banana, (pisang raja) and gold banana (pisang mas). Adding a touch of honey or a scoop of vanilla ice cream to the banana fritters is a must for some. For others, adding sambal roa generates a delicious umame flavour. Sambal roa is made using dried and smoky garfish with chillies and shallots. You can substitute sambal bajak or chilli sauce, although, in my opinion it's not the same.

Serves 4-6

Ingredients:
- 4 ripe kapuk or Cavendish banana, cut into 1cm wide slices
- 50gr all-purpose flour, sieved
- 170gr rice flour, sieved
- 2 eggs, lightly beaten
- 225ml low fat milk
- ½ tsp salt
- 1 tbsp of sugar
- Oil for deep-frying

Directions:
- In a large bowl, mix the flour, salt and sugar.
- Add the lightly beaten eggs and milk little by little, mixing to a silky, smooth finish – take care not to mix too long.
- Add the banana and mix briefly – into the batter
- Heat oil for deep-frying until hot. Use a serving spoon to scoop up the banana batter and cook in the hot oil.
- Cook until golden. Turn the fritters over. Cook for one-two extra minutes then remove from the oil onto a paper kitchen towel to absorb the excess oil.
- Serve warm with a touch of honey, vanilla ice cream or sambal roa, or simply as is.

Palm sugar, white sesame and speculaas bread

ROTI GAMBANG

This is similar to sponge cake with a more dense texture and a unique mini baguette shape. It does not require yeast. Cinnamon is normally added but I replace with my own spiced speculaas mix, which I collaborate together with Javara, an indigenous Indonesia company. It has a really nice caramelized taste from the palm sugar and layers of fragrance from ginger, nutmeg, cloves and cinnamon.

Makes 10 mini baguette shaped bread

Ingredients:
- 300gr strong flour, sieved
- 1 tsp each baking powder and baking soda, sieved
- 1 tbsp speculaas mix
- ½ tsp each of baking powder and baking soda
- 1 tsp of salt
- 75gr butter, melted
- 1 egg, lightly whisked
- 20gr white sesame, roasted
- 150gr palm sugar block, sliced into thin pieces or replaced with 100gr coconut sugar or brown sugar
- 75ml water
- 20gr white sesame, roasted to a golden brown

Directions:
- Put the sliced palm sugar (or coconut sugar or brown sugar) in the pan, add water and cook until you have a honey texture. Strain and set aside.
- Mix all the dried ingredients; flour, baking soda and baking powder, speculaas mix and salt in a large bowl. Make a well in the centre of the flour mixture and crack the eggs into it. Beat the eggs mixture with a fork until smooth. Add the palm sugar syrup. Using the tips of your fingers, mix the eggs, melted butter and palm sugar syrup with the flour, incorporating a little at a time, until everything is combined well into a smooth and silky textured dough.
- Cover the dough with a damp kitchen towel for around 45 minutes until the mixture has risen a little. Knead the dough for another 10 minutes.
- Pre-heat the oven to 160°C. Measure the dough into approximately 40gr and shape into oval shapes. Place onto a lightly buttered baking tray.
- Brush each of the dough with water or milk and sprinkle with white sesame seeds. Bake for around 30-35 minutes or until cooked thoroughly.
- Remove each of the bread from the tray and place on a wire rack to cool. Ready to serve warm or at room temperature.

Gluten-free & vegetarian chocolate brownies with a speculaas twist

COKLAT DAN REMPAH BROWNIES

This is very delicious and easy to make. No one will say no to these delicious warmly spiced brownies with a touch of ginger, cloves, cinnamon, nutmeg and plenty of chocolate and cashew.

Serves 24-28

You need a 35x25cm square baking pan

Ingredients:
- 150gr rice flour
- 50gr sago
- 50gr mung bean flour
- 300gr dark chocolate, chopped
- 200ml coconut oil or vegetable oil
- 300gr coconut sugar (or replace with soft brown sugar)
- 6 eggs
- 300gr roasted cashew, roughly chopped (optional)
- 2 tbsp Javara speculaas spice mix

Directions:
- Pre-heat oven to 170°C.
- Grease the baking pan with butter and line it with greased parchment paper.
- Put the chocolate in a heatproof bowl and set over a saucepan of barely simmering water. Stir until silky smooth and combined well. Remove the bowl from the saucepan and set aside to cool.
- Combine the flour with the spices and salt. Set aside. Whisk the sugar, eggs, speculaas spice mix until combined. Add the melted chocolate and coconut oil or vegetable oil. Combine well.
- Add the flour and cashew and combine well. Don't over mix it.
- Pour the mixture into the prepared baking pan, spread evenly and bake on the middle shelf of the oven for about 30-35 minutes or until set.
- Remove from the oven and leave to cool completely. Slice into 24 or 28 slices and serve with a cup of tea or coffee.

Kelepon

KELEPON

Similar to Japanese mochi which feature the common dessert ingredient of glutinous rice flour. Kelepon are little balls sweetened with palm sugar syrup and coated in juicy, grated coconut. It is best to use soft coconut not old and dried coconut.

Makes 24 Pieces

Ingredients:

- 200g glutinous rice flour
- 50ml water
- 100g palm sugar, shaved
- 1 coconut, flesh grated
- 2 litres water for boiling

Directions:

- Mix the glutinous rice flour with the water. The texture will be very soft.
- Put 1 dessert spoon of the mixture into your palm and flatten it. Put 1 tsp of palm sugar on the dough and roll it to make a ball. Make sure the sugar stays inside the dough. Continue making rice balls until all the dough has been used.
- Bring the water to the boil. Reduce the heat to medium and put the rice balls into the boiling water, 10 at a time. When cooked, the rice balls float to the surface.
- Remove with a strainer and roll each rice ball in grated coconut.
- Best served warm.

Last minute avocado brûlée

ALPUKAT DENGAN SAUS COKLAT

This idea is inspired by a traditional Indonesian avocado and chocolate smoothie. In this version, the texture is like a mousse. If you need a dessert at the last minute, this is it! This Brûlée has the texture of mousse and should be made no more than half an hour before serving.

Serves 4-6

- 2 avocados
- 200ml full cream milk
- 3 tbsp sugar
- 125g dark chocolate, 70% cocoa (melted)
- 50g chilled butter
- 4 small glasses

Directions:
- Melt the chocolate and butter in a bowl over a pan of simmering water. Make sure the bowl sits nicely on top of the pan and doesn't touch the water.
- Cut the avocados in half lengthways and remove the stones.
- Scoop out the flesh of the avocado and mix in a blender.
- Add the sugar and milk to the avocado blend and mix for a few minutes until you have a mousse-like texture.
- Swirl the melted chocolate around the inside of the glasses.
- Pour the avocado mixture into the glasses and swirl more chocolate on top. Serve.

Tips: I have found that keeping avocado in the refrigerator for a long time is not a good idea, as the avocado takes on a strange taste.

Steamed rice chocolate cake with grated coconut

KUE PUTU COKLAT

The idea for this recipe emanated from the kue putu street snack of rice flour, extract of pandan leaves and palm sugar - used here as a centre for the cake. For something different, I have replaced the pandan and palm sugar syrup by substituting chocolate. It is a great companion for coconut. The classic kue putu has a unique squat tube shape arising from the bamboo mold. A small ramekin works well for this cake. Alas there is no substitute for the bamboo steam whistles of genuine kue putu sellers wandering the city backstreets and alleys. Sadly this distinctive sound is beginning to disappear.

Makes 10 small ramekins

Ingredients:
- 375gr rice flour
- 100gr chocolate chips or grated chocolate
- 2 tbsp cocoa powder
- 50gr sugar
- 250ml low fat milk or coconut milk or water for lighter taste if preferred
- ½ freshly grated coconut (around 200gr) or 150gr desiccated coconut, use some for garnish
- 1½ tsp salt

For the Salted Chocolate Coulis:
- 100gr chocolate with 70% cocoa
- 25ml butter
- 100ml cream

Directions:
- Combine the rice flour with 1 tsp of salt, sugar, cocoa powder and mix well.
- Add milk a little by little until the mixture is silky and dense.
- Divide the mixture into five equal portions, shape into balls, steam for 25 minutes and set aside to cool.
- Season the grated ginger with salt and mix well.
- Break the rice flour balls into small pieces and mix in salted coconut.
- Prepare the ramekin. Smear with a thin layer of butter.
- Lightly press the rice flour mixture into the ramekin to around 1cm thickness and add a generous layer of chocolate chips, then cover with more rice flour mixture. Repeat until all ramekins are filled. Steam the ramekins for around 25 minutes.
- Remove the ramekin from the steamer. Sprinkle with fresh coconut and serve warm.

Es pallu butung with strawberry granita, strawberry compote and thick young coconut sauce

ES PALLU BUTUNG

It has very refreshing taste with fresh strawberries and a light and delicious young coconut flavour. A perfect combination with steamed banana.

Serves 10-12

- 5-6 'kapok' or 3 ripe plantains
- 2-3 tbsp of condensed milk (optional)

Ingredients for Strawberry Granita
- 450gr fresh ripe strawberries, hulled and cut into halves
- 175gr sugar

- 3 tbsp lime juice
- 600 ml water
- 2 ice cream containers with 500ml capacity each

Ingredients for the Thick Young Coconut Sauce
- 150ml coconut cream (preferably homemade but you can use tinned coconut if you prefer)
- coconut flesh from 4 young coconuts

Ingredients for the Strawberry Compote
- 600gr fresh strawberries, half washed and quartered and the other half blended to make juice
- 4 tbsp sugar
- 50ml lime juice
- 100ml water
- 1 vanilla pod, sliced lengthwise, vanilla seeds scraped and set aside

Directions:
- Simply steam the banana with the skin until soft.
- To prepare the granita. Put the strawberry in a colander and briefly rinse. Dry with a kitchen towel.
- Put the strawberries in a food processor. Add sugar, puree then add water and lime juice. Blend again for a few seconds.
- Pour the mixture into an ice cream container, cover with the lid and put into the freezer for 2 hours. By that time, the mixture should have started to freeze around the edges and the base of the container.
- Take a large fork and mix contents for a consistent granita then re-cover and repeat until the entire mixture is frozen. Leave overnight.
- For the coconut sauce: simply put the young coconut flesh and coconut cream into a blender and blend until it becomes a very smooth and very thick creamy texture. Transfer the mixture into a bowl and put in the refrigerator.
- For the strawberry compote. Put all the ingredients into a pan, bring to the boil and turn the heat into low-medium until all the sugar is dissolved and the vanilla infused. Simmer for 20 minutes or until the texture approaches a syrupy texture. Set aside to cool.
- To serve, prepare 10-12 large glasses or small glass bowls. Put scoops of the granita into the glasses, add 5-7 slices of banana and a tbsp of thick coconut sauce. Drizzle with strawberry compote. Garnish with mint leaves. Serve immediately.

Jellied leaves and coconut ice cream

ES CINCAU

Known locally as grass jelly ice, the jelly is made by squeezing cincau green leaves with water until all the extract of the leaves comes out. It is 100% natural and suitable for vegans or vegetarians. The taste of the coconut ice cream is delicate and light as there are no eggs but just pure young coconut flesh.

Serves 4
You need 4 small ramekins or glasses as molds

Ingredients
For the grass jelly:
- 250ml milk
- 60 cincau leaves or around 30gr

For the coconut ice cream:
- 3 whole young coconuts with soft texture (not gelatinous)

For the cashew brittle:
- 100 gr unsalted roasted cashew, roughly ground
- 100gr sugar

Other ingredients:
- 1 papaya chilli (large red chilli), remov the seeds and chop finely

Directions:
- For the jelly: Wash the cincau leaves with mineral water and set aside. Put 250ml milk into a bowl and with your hand, start to squeeze the leaves in the milk for 15 minutes. The milk turns green and becomes a little thick. Strain the liquid with a fine strainer into a small jug. Then transfer the mixture into individual ramekins or any mold. Put the ramekins in the refrigerator for at least 4 hours or overnight.
- For the coconut ice cream: Put the young coconut flesh into a blender and process until the mixture turns silky and smooth. Transfer the mixture into a container and put it in the freezer to set but stir the mixture every hour for the first 3 hours to have a smooth textured ice cream.
- To make the cashew brittle: In a medium saucepan, add the sugar into the pan and heat over medium flame until the sugar and change to caramel. Do not stir at all. Once the sugar reaches the desired caramel colour, remove from the heat. Immediately add the ground cashews, stir quickly and mix well.
- Transfer the mixture onto parchment or baking paper, spreading it quickly to an even thickness. Make sure it is not too thick. Allow the brittle to cool completely, then break into small pieces or put into a strong food processor.
- To serve, spread the cashew brittle on the middle of each serving plate. Remove the cincau from the mold, discard the liquid and place on the left side of the plate. Add ice cream on the other side and sprinkle the chillies around to give a nice colour and interesting taste. Serve immediately.

Sweet potatoes and banana cooked with palm sugar and coconut

KOLAK

Kolak is a classic Indonesian drink that is especially popular during the fasting month. The sweet, comforting drink is the perfect thing for an empty stomach when breaking the fast at sundown.

Kolak is usually made with sweet potato and/or banana, or mung beans, pandan leaves, palm sugar and coconut cream. It has a delicious sweet flavour with a touch of sourness from the banana.

Serves 8-10

Ingredients:
- 300 gr sweet potatoes, preferably orange in color, peeled and cubed
- 300gr or 2 large pisang Ambon, or Cavendish bananas (300 gr), peeled and cubed
- 100ml of palm sugar syrup, made of 150gr roughly chopped palm sugar and 50ml
- 2 cinnamon sticks or 2 pandan leaves, roughly chopped
- 900ml water
- 400ml coconut cream
- 50 gr roasted almond flake
- Half a tsp of salt

Direction:
- Make palm sugar syrup by boiling the sugar and water together, simmer for 7 minutes, until the sugar is melted, strain and set aside.
- Boil the sweet potatoes, 900 milliliters water and pandan leaves or cinnamon sticks, then simmer until tender.
- Add the banana and palm sugar syrup tand simmer for around 10 minutes.
- Add the coconut milk and simmer for another 5 minutes. Remove from the heat, cool to room temperature, then transfer into a big bowl and refrigerate to chill.
- To serve, place in 8-10 serving glasses, sprinkle with roasted almond flakes and garnish with cinnamon sticks.

Red and green bean ice cream

ES KRIM KACANG MERAH DAN KACANG HIJAU

This red bean ice cream is inspired from Manadonese *es kacang merah* which is basically cooked red bean, condensed milk and plenty of shaved ice. Sometimes durian is added. Simply replace the red beans with mung beans to make green bean ice cream. Both are delicious.

Makes 1 litre

- 300g red kidney beans, soaked overnight
- 1 litre water for boiling
- 150g sugar
- 225ml cream
- 225ml full cream milk
- 5 egg yolks
- 1 vanilla pod, sliced in half

Directions:
- Rinse the beans and soak over night. Discard the water and cook for 1½ hours in a fresh litre of water or until the beans are soft. Drain the water, and set the beans a side to cool. Lightly beat egg yolks in a bowl.
- Combine the milk and the cream in a saucepan.
- Cut the vanilla pod in half lengthwise, scrape out the seeds, add seeds and pod to the milk mixture. Put the pan on a low heat and whisk until the milk is simmering.
- Still whisking, pour the milk mixture into the egg yolks.
- Place the bowl over barely simmering water and keep stirring until the mixture is thick enough to coat the back of a wooden spoon. Remove from the heat and cool completely.
- Pour the mixture into a blender, add the cooked beans and run it for 3-4 minutes, but no longer, to preserve a chunky texture.
- Freeze in an ice cream maker

Young coconut ice

ES KELAPA MUDA

Young coconuts are normally available in the traditional markets around Jakarta, however it is a pity that ice cubes are often added to the mixture, which dilutes the flavour of pure coconut water. Add palm sugar syrup to experience something different. You can keep coconut water in the refrigerator for only one or two days.

1 whole young coconut water and the flesh is sufficient for one or two persons

Direction:
- At home scrape out the young flesh from the coconut- with a tablespoon, place in a glass jar and separately store the water in a container
- Put flesh and water in the refrigerator for 1-2 hours before serving
- For a different taste, add 1-2 tbsp of palm sugar syrup (see page 39)

Guava granite

ES SERUT JAMBU BIJI

I adore the beuatiful colour and fragrance of pink guava. This recipe is easy to make and delicous.

Ingredients:
* ½ kg guava, cut into half, seeds scooped out and discarded (peel the skin if you want to your sorbet to have strong pink colour), you should end up with about 700 gr flesh
* 200 gr sugar
* Juice of 2-3 limes
* 1½ cups of water

Directions:
* Combine the water and sugar, bring to a simmer until sugar is dissolved.
* Pour the mixture into a bowl and set aside at room temperature.
* Place the guava in a blender, plus half of the sugar syrup. Puree.
* Add the rest of the sugar syrup and lime juice, mix well.
* Pour the mixture into a suitable container and place in the freezer.
* When the edges freeze (after 20-30 minutes, depending on your freezer), scrape them off and stir the ice crystals into the liquid part.
* Allow to freeze completely.
* Remove container 15-20 minutes before serving.

Pineapple, ginger and chilli sorbet

ES SERUT NANAS, JAHE DAN CABE

This combination offers a refreshing taste from the pineapple, ginger and chillies. A perfect sorbet for a summer day with a little spicy kick to it.

Ingredients:

- 2 pineapples or 1kg pineapple flesh peeled, eyes removed, core discarded, chopped roughly
- 150 gr caster (superfine) sugar
- 7cm of fresh ginger, peeled and finely grated
- 2 red curly chillies, finely chopped
- juice of 2-3 limes
- 2 egg whites

Directions:

- Place the pineapple, sugar, lime juice, chillies and grated ginger into a food processor or power blender. Process until the mixture is creamy. Strain the mixture through a fine sieve into a big bowl.
- Whip eggwhites until soft and creamy using an electric hand mixer.
- Take one big spoon of whipped white egg and fold into the pineapple mixture. Repeat until all the whipped egg is incorporated.
- Transfer the mixture into a container suitable for freezing and place in freezer
- When the edges freeze (after 20-30 minutes, depending on your freezer), scrape them off and stir the ice crystals into the liquid part.
- Repeat every 20 or 30 minutes or until you have a semi-frozen mixture.
- Allow to freeze completely. Remove container 15-20 minutes before serving.

Index

Places names are shown in bold italic. Some ingredients and recipes in Indonesian names shown in italic.

A
Avocado
  Last minute avocado brulee, 201

B
Banana, 27
  Banana friters, 195
  Banana Kolak Gelato, 206
Bandung dumplings with spicy
  peanut sauce, 98
Barbequed King prawns with
  Borneo mango salad, 94
Betawi Omelette with ginger and
  turmeric consommé, 54
Beef
  Beef stew Betawi style, 73
  Beef croquettes with simple
    salad, 154
  Beef stew with carrots and
    potatoes, 157
  Black nut beef stew, 166
  Slow-cooked beef with
    caramelized shallots and
    spices, 154
  West Sumatera dried beef
    curry, 149
Black Pepper, 27
Bumbu, 34

C
Candlenuts, 27
Cardamom, 27
Chicken
  Acehnese fried chicken with
    curry and pandan leaves, 161
  Aromatic white chicken curry, 158
  Chicken pop cooked in coconut
    water with a modern bun
    twist, 165
  Chicken Fried Rice with chillies
    and vegetables, 105
  Chicken curry with pineapple, 164
  Classic chicken satay with
    a peanut and lime sauce, 170
  Ketoprak with griddled breast
    chicken, 51
  Roasted chicken, Jakarta
    style, 74
  Roasted chicken, Lombok
    style, 162
Chillies, 27
Chinese Lemon, 28
Cinnamon, 27
Cloves, 27
Coconut
  Coconut cream, 27
  Coconut Crème Brûlée, 193

Coconut milk, 27
Coconut tart, 191
Green pancakes with coconut, 190
Steamed rice chocolate cake
  with grated coconut, 202
Sweet mashed cassava with
  grated coconut, 194
Young Coconut Ice, 205
Corn Cakes with Tomato
  Salsa , 129

D
Drinks
  Carrot, pineapple, ginger
    juice, 180
  Mango juice, 182
  Soursop juice, 181
Duck
  Acehnese duck curry, 150

E
Es pallu butung with strawberry
  granita, strawberry compote and
  thick young coconut sauce, 203

F
Fennel, 27
Fenugreek, 27

Fish
  Acehnese Barramundi
    fillet curry with a twist, 89
  Angel hair with Manadonese
    mixed seafood woku blanga
    sauce, 86
  Fillet of white snapper arsik
    from North Sumatera, 92
  Fish fillet with turmeric and
    chillies sauce, 78
  Grilled Fish with lime and
    chillies, 90
  Raw Tuna with calamansi, chilli
    and kemangi, 91
  Tagliatelle with Manado tuna
    "rica-rica", 93
  Tekwan with red mackerel and
    prawn, 85
  White snapper fillet with
    black nut sauce served with
    pasta, 77
  Whole steamed coral trout with
    chillies and ginger sauce, 81
Fried rice, 103
  Chicken fried rice with chillies
    and vegetables, 105
  Fried rice with goat meat spices
    and sweet soya sauce, 108
  Padang Pesto Fried Rice With
    shrimps, 106
  Seafood fried rice, 107
  Village Fried Rice, 104
Fried tempeh and tofu, 145

G
Galangal, 27
Ginger, 28
  Aromatic ginger, 28
  Carrot, pineapple and ginger
    juice, 180
  Ginger tea, 187
Gluten-free and vegetarian
  chocolate brownies with a
  speculaas twist, 198
Goat curry with natural
  yoghurt, 165
Guava granite, 210

I
Ice cream
  Red and Green Bean
    ice cream, 208
  Jellied leaves and coconut
    ice cream, 205

J
Juice
  Carrot, pineapple and ginger
    juice, 184
  Mango juice, 186
  Soursop juice, 185

K
Kaffir lime, 28
Kelepon, 200
Klapertaart, 187

L
Lemon grass, 28
Leaf
  Curry leaf, 28
  Lime leaf, 28
  Pandan leaf, 31
  Turmeric leaf, 31
Leaves Jelly, Coconut Ice
  Cream, Coconut Sugar,
  Cashew and Chillies, 201
Lime, 28

M
Mango, 24
  Juice, 182
Mangosteen, 28
Manadonese risotto, 134
Mini savoury minced beef
  omelette with pastry, 133

N
Noodles
  Acehnese fried noodles
    with prawn and mixed
    vegetable, 111
  Laksa Medan, 119
  Meatballs with rice noodles, 112
  Noodles chicken, 114
  Stir-fried noodles, chicken, eggs
    and sweet soy a sauce, 116
Nutmeg, 28

O

Onde-onde (see *kelepon*), 196
Otak-otak with Cucumber & Carrots, 97

P

Palm sugar, 28
  Palm sugar, white sesame and speculaas bread, 197
  Syrup, 39
Pandan (see screwpine leaf), 31
Papaya, 28
Paste, 34
  Green paste, 34
  Red paste, 34
  White paste, 34
  Yellow paste, 34
Pineapple, 28
  Pineapple, Ginger and Chilli Sorbet, 211
Pickles, 37
Prawn Laksa, 67
Pumpkin, 31

R

Red Bean, 208
Rice
  Fragrant rice cooked with coconut milk, ginger and lemon grass, 69
  Fragrant rice with spicy coconut dressing, 68
  Rice Pannacota with palm sugar syrup and cashew, 188
  Yellow rice, 109
Roasted tempeh and tofu with shallots, soya and spicy gravy, 141

S

Salad
  Ketoprak with griddled chicken breast, 51
  Mixed vegetables and fruits served with a spicy, sour and sweet sauce, 47
  Mixed vegetable salad, tofu, potatoes and tempeh, 48
  Mixed vegetable salad with spicy and zingy peanut sauce, 130
  Mixed vegetable wedding salad, 43
  Tropical fruit salad served with sweet, spicy and tangy tamarind and palm sugar dressing, 44
  Salted fish, 31
Sambal, 35
Sate Republic, 166
  Beef Sate Padang with spices, 180
  Classic chicken Satay with peanut, chillies, soya and lime, 174
  Goat Sate Tanah Abang, 177
  Minced seafood sate from Bali, 173
  Pork Satay with Chilli and Ginger Paste, 178
  Sweet and aromatic beef sate marrangi from West Java, 181
Star anis, 31
Soto
  Jakarta Noodles Soto, 62
  Soto Betawi with a twist, 61
Soup
  East Java clear spiced chicken soup, 120
  Goat carrot and potato soup, 63
  Hot and sour prawn soup with asam sunti, 125
  Makassar beef soup with fermented soya, 123
  Oxtail Soup, 64
  Sour and spicy fish soup with pineapple, 124
Soya sauce, 31

T

Tamarind, 31
Thick pancakes, 192
Turmeric, 31
Twice cooked tofu soya cake with tamarind and coriander, 144

U

Urap, 138

V

Vegetable
  Vegetable curry, soft boiled egg with rice cake, 52
  Mixed vegetable curry , 137
  Mixed vegetables with young tamarind broth, 56
  Mixed vegetables with sambal terasi, 141
  Roasted eggplants with chillies, 140

W

Water apple, 31
White Pepper, 31

Y

Yellow rice, 109
Young coconut ice, 205

Acknowledgements

This very special book would not have been possible without a team who gave great support. My thanks go to the Komunika team who helped me with the design of the book and the photography and also my team in the kitchen especially my sister Esty who gave considerable support from the beginning of this project.

I also want to thank my family, friends and fellow chefs from many establishments who collaborated with me in the last 5 years and friends that have been involved in my work. Some of the recipes from this book has been published in Jakarta Globe and Now Jakarta to which I contributed for many years. It has given me a great pleasure to meet many street food vendors and market vendors during my research.

Also a huge thanks to my dear friend Joy Karabaczek who helped me to edit this book. I would like to thank my family and many friends for their great encouragement. Last but not least, thanks to my dearest husband Nick and my two great sons, Chris and Jeremy for making my life so colourful.